Conf
Asser
Self E

A series of 12 sessions for secondary school students

Tina Rae

Lucky Duck is more than a publishing house and training agency. George Robinson and Barbara Maines founded the company in the 1980's when they worked together as a head and psychologist developing innovative strategies to support challenging students.

They have an international reputation for their work on bullying, self-esteem, emotional literacy and many other subjects of interest to the world of education.

George and Barbara have set up a regular news-spot on the website. Twice yearly these items will be printed as a newsletter. If you would like to go on the mailing list to receive this then please contact us:

e-mail newsletter@luckyduck.co.uk   website www.luckyduck.co.uk

ISBN 1873942 97 4

www.luckyduck.co.uk

Designed by Helen Weller
Printed by Antony Rowe Limited

© Tina Rae 2000
Reprinted January 2001, October 2001, July 2002, June 2003, March 2004

Contents

How to use the CD-ROM

The CD-ROM contains a PDF file labelled 'Worksheets.pdf' which contains worksheets for each session in this resource. You will need Acrobat Reader version 3 or higher to view and print these pages. The document is set up to print to A4 but you can enlarge the pages to A3 by increasing the output percentage at the point of printing using the page set-up settings for your printer.

To photocopy the worksheets directly from this book, set your photocopier to enlarge by 125% and align the edge of the page to be copied against the leading edge of the the copier glass (usually indicated by an arrow).

Introduction and Background

This programme is designed to be used in the Secondary phase and is specifically aimed at students who exhibit low self-esteem, low levels of confidence and an inability to assert themselves in a positive and appropriate way. These difficulties will often be part of more general emotional and behavioural difficulties which will frequently have a detrimental effect upon learning and or the development of basic skills. This course consequently aims to support such students in developing the skills and strategies they need in order to cope more effectively in both the school and home context.

Recent research has focused upon how low self-esteem can be further developed and enhanced and how schools as institutions can aid students in the process of developing appropriate social skills and a positive self image. (Rutter 1991, Goleman 1995). Students who exhibit an appropriate level of self-esteem will usually have experienced some success in social situations and received appropriate levels of reinforcement and praise. They will generally have no difficulty in coping with a variety of social situations and will be able to form relationships with confidence, responding positively to constructive criticism and have the confidence to effect change. Those who exhibit low self-esteem will tend to feel worthless, useless and unloved and consequently exhibit defensive and aggressive behaviours towards others. They are generally caught up in a cycle of negative thinking which can initially appear impossible to break free from.

Social pressures and in particular, peer pressures are certainly contributing factors in reinforcing levels of self-esteem and confidence. High school students appear to be experiencing very real pressures to 'look right' , (generally slim, wearing trendy clothes and having the 'right' hairstyle etc) to be reasonably successful academically (but without appearing to be a 'boffin') and to be popular and 'wanted' by both female and male friends. Such pressures not only reinforce personal inadequacies but can also contribute to specific behaviours such as social withdrawal, disaffected and disruptive behaviours or even refusal to attend school. Such disaffected behaviours can lead to both short-term and permanent exclusion from school:

'children who become disaffected fail to gain the educational and social skills they need to succeed in adult life, while at the same time using up a disproportionate share of the resources available to educate all children'. (DFEE 1999).

Recent government initiatives include a commitment to provide funding in order to reduce truancy and exclusion levels by one third by the year 2002. This has lead many schools to re-evaluate their systems and how to develop appropriate strategies in order to address the needs of disaffected students. Schools will need to ensure that they effectively manage a preventative approach supporting students with emotional and behavioural difficulties which includes identifying needs and implementing programmes of support at the earliest opportunity.

Consequently, support services and LEA's clearly need to adopt preventative approaches in working with these groups of students. The underachievement of boys is necessarily and evidently a considerable problem with boys 3 times more likely to permanently excluded than girls (Hinds, 98). However, there is also growing concern at the number of girls exhibiting aggressive and confrontational behaviours and the inability to cope effectively in all social contexts.

A Preventative Approach

This programme aims to provide teachers with a preventative approach which will enable students to develop appropriate skills and strategies. It is aimed at students who are experiencing emotional and or behavioural difficulties as a direct result of low levels of self-esteem, confidence and an inability to assert themselves in a positive manner. It is hoped that schools will have already addressed their problems with the students concerned and naturally that the schools Pastoral and SEN Systems will have worked closely in partnership with Parents. Such work may have included regular liaison with parents, monitoring systems, mentoring schemes, individual behaviour plans and perhaps some outside agency involvement. Students will have been identified and placed at Stages 2 or 3 of the school based process of assessment for special educational needs. The focus is on helping students to identify and recognise the causes and roots of low self-esteem and confidence and to develop appropriate coping strategies and skills with which to operate in an assertive, confident and positive manner in all social situations and contexts. This course is designed to be used with a group of between 6-10 students. The group can be gender mixed or single sex as deemed appropriate by course tutors or as dictated by the nature of the school itself ie.single sex or mixed.

Objectives

The lessons in this programme have been designed to meet the following objectives:

- to enable students to develop and practice the skills of positive thinking
- to increase self-esteem / self concept
- to understand and experience the feeling of respect.
- to understand the difference between aggression and assertion
- to develop and practice assertiveness skills
- to encourage an understanding of how others view us and how this can / may impact upon our self-esteem
- to begin to develop an understanding of what friendship means and the skills needed to be a good friend
- to enable students to further develop and appreciate the perspectives of others ie. develop empathy
- to recognise that we all have the right to be who we are and to accepted by others
- to develop joint problem solving skills within a supportive framework
- to enable students to identify feelings of stress and to develop appropriate personal coping strategies
- to increase students' levels of confidence in social situations and interactions
- to develop staff awareness of a range of strategies to manage challenging behaviour and emotional difficulties
- to raise staff awareness as to how they can develop their own skills in managing students with emotional and behavioural difficulties (including differentiation of the curriculum ñ both social and academic)

- to enable all staff, as a team, to review current practice and to work together in developing appropriate initiatives which will promote the inclusion of such at risk students.

Structure of the Programme

Introductory Session

One to one interviews with students who will be included in the Programme. The interviews adopt a Brief Therapy approach in order to identify Needs and develop appropriate targets.

Session 1

Completion of Self Esteem Rating Questionnaire. Students complete this questionnaire which aims to identify current levels of self esteem. Specific targets are then formulated and reinforced via a Self-Profile. Group Rules are set in this session.

Session2

Identifying Negative Thinking. Looking at Triggers to negative thinking and how this affects our self-esteem.

Session 3

Identification of 'Positive Points' and practising positive thinking skills. Turning 'negative notes' into 'positive points'.

Session 4

Using 'Mirror Talk' and 'Top Talk' techniques in order to practice and develop skills of positive thinking. Identifying qualities of a best friend.

Session 5

Identification of Negatives which can be Changed into Positives. Students formulate Individual Action Plans. Looking at how we can support each other in making changes.

Session 6

Learning to accept and respect yourself. Understanding the concept of respect.

Session 7

Coping with stress. Identifying situations/specific problems/people that can induce stress. Students develop and practice self help strategies.

Session 8

Understanding the difference between being assertive and being aggressive. Practising assertive behaviour via Role Play. Use of Video and Situation Cards.

Session 9

Identifying triggers to anger and how to respond assertively to anger. Practising assertive responses to anger via Role Play. Use of Video and Problem Page Scenarios.

Session 10

Giving and taking Compliments ñ practising both skills. Reinforcements of 'Top Talk' and 'Mirror Talk'.

Session 11

Identifying and accepting Positive Criticism. Using Positive Criticism to affect change.

Session 12

Course Review and Evaluation. Going for a better you and looking to the Future.

Each session provides course tutors with a set of photocopiable worksheets / resources for students to make use of. Where the resources may not be entirely appropriate for both male and female students, additional alternative worksheets have been provided. Clearly, whatever the gender make up of the group, tutors simply photocopy the appropriate resources / worksheets. Any need to make use of alternative worksheets is indicated in the lesson plans.

IEPs

This Programme can supply the basis of a whole school approach towards building self-esteem, confidence and positive behaviour. It aims to promote the inclusion of students who are experiencing emotional and behavioural difficulties and supports the belief that effective support systems with clear systems and agreed strategies can affect change. Within such a framework, students should be able to begin to develop the skills they need in order to cope effectively in the school and home contexts. This Programme may also form part of a whole school approach to training staff to respond effectively and appropriately to students who are experiencing these kinds of problems. There are clearly opportunities to share good practice and work that is being carried out within the group can inform student's IEP's (Individual Education Plan) or IBP's (Individual Behaviour Plan) and ensure the formulation of appropriate and meaningful targets.

Mentoring Schemes and Partnerships with Parents

It might be appropriate to also implement a Mentoring Scheme which can run alongside the CAS Course. Students can have the opportunity to work alongside a significant / trusted adult with the focus on reviewing progress, formulating appropriate targets and reinforcement and further development of effective coping strategies. Clearly, the Mentor would need to be updated on the on-going work within the CAS Course Group and liaison time would need to be built in to any individual programme of support. Once the CAS Course has been completed the continuation of any such Mentoring scheme would ensure that appropriate support is on-going and still available to the student. The Mentor would also be able to ensure a link with Parents / carers. This is clearly essential if the support programme is to be implemented successfully.

A Way Forward

Currently, much of the good practice which is in place in the Primary Sector with regards to the emotional curriculum is not being transferred to Key Stages 3 and 4. Students who have experienced lessons in emotional awareness training, Circle Time approaches and a variety of listening and problem solving sessions via the PSHE curriculum are suddenly confronted with sketchy, if any, such similar support. All these techniques can offer students the opportunity to develop the social and emotional skills they need which are clearly essential if they are to cope effectively in all contexts. This programme aims to act as a starting point for schools to develop their own approaches in working with older students on the development of such skills. Clearly, any schemes will need to be developed in the light of individual schools' needs and priorities. The CAS Course does not in any sense claim to be a cure-all for students exhibiting low self-esteem, low confidence levels and inability to make use of positive assertion skills. There is no easy answer or solution to such a wide range of emotional and behavioural difficulties. What this course can and hopefully does do is to begin to ask pertinent questions and open up the debate as to how we can best support such students.

It is extremely important that students who have been involved in the group continue to have access to support once the course is finished. The use of some form of Mentoring Scheme and or further involvement of Parents / Carers in working with the school to develop appropriate support systems will be necessary in terms of ensuring that the student feels and is supported. Outside Agencies may also be called on in order to build on the work that has taken place within the group. The CAS Course Action Plan and the Success Check List should allow for provision of an individual profile of each student's needs. Clearly, whatever decisions are made, the key to successful provision is flexibility of approach. It may well be that the curriculum will need to be adapted or reduced for some students and individual programmes of work experience, alternative course placements and access to emotional support (counselling) planned and delivered.

For many of the individual students who have been targeted via this particular course, there will have been a definite increase in their access to real 'Listening time'. A Mentoring scheme would at least continue to ensure a weekly one to one session during which students could discuss problems encountered and ensure that they have a confidential forum in which to problem solve and further develop the skills that they need. This approach could also form the basis of a whole school policy and approach to listening time and this would necessarily have resource and training implications ie. training in counselling skills, review of PSHE curriculum and creation of specific listening environments.

Hopefully, whatever decision is taken with regards to 'the way forward', schools will aim to ensure that their curriculum ñ academic, social and emotional, in both flexible and carefully designed so as to ensure the inclusion and development of all students. It is vital not to forget that

'Where schools are rigid in their academic labelling of pupils, pupils tend to fall into polarised groups: those who are successful and who, therefore, gain self-esteem from the school experience, against those who are the failures and who find school a source of rejection and humiliation. The former develop pro-school values and attitudes, while the latter are likely to reject school and form anti-school sub-cultures' (Hargreaves, 1967).

Hopefully, this Programme can and will reinforce the need for such flexibility and provide the initial prompt for schools to review and further develop practice and resources for students who appear to lack the necessary skills to cope effectively ñ socially, emotionally and academically.

Success Criteria

It is hoped that the success of the CAS Course can be measured in the following areas:

- removing the risk of students becoming school refusers
- removing the risk of exclusion
- prompting the school to reflect upon its practices and how they may impact upon student's behaviour, self-esteem and social and emotional development
- causing the school to assess the appropriateness of the curriculum and to identify any need to develop further opportunities to address the social and emotional curriculum
- a review of Policies on Bullying, Self-Esteem and Behaviour management in order to further develop more inclusive whole school approaches
- to critically look at teacher's expectations of behaviour and emotional development in students and to identify training needs in the areas of cultural, gender, class and emotional awareness
- to enable students to develop an awareness and understanding of their own feelings, attitudes and behaviours
- to increase student's ability to reflect upon their own feelings and behaviours and to recognise negative and positive patterns
- to increase self-esteem
- to increase confidence
- to develop and practice assertiveness skills
- for students to understand the difference between assertiveness and aggression and to understand and cope assertively with positive criticism
- to improve and further develop empathy and listening skills
- to further develop self-help strategies in order to cope with negative thoughts, stress, uncomfortable feelings and situation and to understand and make use of techniques taught in the CAS Course
- to develop the ability to transfer the skills taught into a variety of social contexts.

References

DfEE 1997 Excellence for All Children : Meeting SEN.

DfEE 1999 Social Inclusion : Pupil Support.

George,E.,Iveson, C, & Rathner,H. (1990) Problem to Solution: Brief therapy with individuals and families, London. Brief Therapy Publication.

Goleman, D. (1995) Emotional Intelligence. Why it can matter more than I.Q.   London – Bloomsbury.

Hargreaves, D. (1967) Social Relations in a Secondary School, RKP: London.

Lethem, J. (1994) Moved to Tears, Moved to Action: solution focussed brief therapy with women and children.   London, Brief Therapy Publication.

Moseley.J. & Gillibrand.E. (1995) She Who Dares Wins.   Thorsons.

Rhodes, J. & Ajmal.Y. (1995) Solution Focussed Thinking in Schools Behaviour, reading and organisation.   B.T. Press London.

Rutter,M. (1991) Pathways from Children to Adult Life.
Pastoral Care in Education Vol 9. No.3.

Shazer, S. (1988) Clues: Investigating Solutions in Brief Therapy.
New York: Norton.

Warden, D. & Christie, D. (1997) Teaching Social Behaviour
David Fulton Publishers.

Introductory Session

Initial 1:1 interview making use of a Brief
therapy approach in order to identify needs
and set appropriate goals

Introductory Session

One to one session with individual students.
Individual Session I hour

This introductory session consists of a one to one interview between each individual student and the course tutor. The interview should last approximately I hour and should enable the student to focus upon what actually works as opposed to what is going wrong ie. the development of a collaborative ethos. The main aim of the session is to aid the student in defining some achievable goals in clarifying what practical resources / strategies are required in order to achieve these goals.

The interview will need to take place in a quiet and comfortable room and the students should be made aware of the 'confidential' nature of the interview ie. their views, thoughts and feelings will not be fed back to Staff / Parents / Carers unless at the request of the individual student. An obvious exception to this rule would be if students disclosed themselves to be at risk. Course tutor(s) would certainly need to clarify the latter point with the students prior to the start of the interview.

The interview follows a solution focused brief therapy approach which focuses upon the development of solutions as opposed to the exploration of problems. Hopefully, the session should allow for some quality time in which the course tutor(s) and student can begin to build a positive relationship. The tutor(s) will record student responses in note form on the I:I interview format.

Part 1

Part 1 of the form focuses on the following questions:
- What is currently going well for the student at school and any reasons for this?
- What is currently not going quite so well a school and any ideas as to why this is so?
- What is currently going well at home and any reasons for this?
- What is currently not going quite so well at home and any ideas as to why this is so?
- Any ideas the student has as to what kind of help / support she might need. Ie. What would actually help?

Part 2

In this part of the interview the student is asked the 'miracle question'. Students are required to imagine themselves in a situation in which all their problems and negative feelings / difficulties are 'solved'. They are all asked to describe a 'perfect' day in which everything goes well (at home and at school). The question is presented in the following way:

'Imagine that you go to bed tonight and a miracle happens! Someone or something waves a magic wand over you and all your problems and difficulties are solved. You wake up to the perfect day both at home and at school. What is different? Have a think. How does your day begin and then go on? Talk through what happens on this ideal / magic day?

The reason behind presenting this Miracle question is to enable the students to begin to visualise 'life without the problem'. (de Shazer, 1988, Furman & Ahola, 1992). Once students begin to talk about life 'without the problem' , it is hoped that they can begin to formulate suggestions and ideas as to how they might begin to make changes. They should also be more able to identify and formulate appropriate and achievable personal goals.

The Scaling Activity next aims to provide a visual image by which the students can clarify where they feel they 'are at' and where and how they would like to move on from this point. These solution focused procedures adopted in the 1:1 initial interview are described by Rhodes & Ajmal in their book 'Solution Focused Thinking in Schools'. The reasons for adopting such an approach is made explicit in the following statements:

'In supporting students, teachers and parents in their wish to change what is happening, we have found no model of approaching behavioural difficulties more useful and flexible than solution focused thinking. It enables a different story to be told, one which emphasises the skills, strengths and resources of those involved'.

Rhodes, J & Ajmal, Y (1995) p.55

When tutor(s) ask the Miracle question they need to emphasise with students that such an ideal / magic day does not preclude them from attending school – the idea is for them to describe school as they would like it to be. Once responses to this question have been recorded, students will then be in a position to answer the following question:

'What is different to a 'usual' day?' The main aim of this activity is to identify and clarify the differences in order to then pin point what changes need to be made. A basic list can then be drawn up, alongside detailing the resources that the individual student will need in order to successfully implement the change process.

Some Examples

Yasmin – aged 13

Yasmin said that when she woke up in the morning her mum didn't even have time to speak to her because she was rushing to get out to work. Yasmin said that she felt as though her mum was angry at her and just didn't like her enough to talk to her. After thinking further she thought that her mum was probably stressed because she had too much to do and Yasmin wasn't helping by getting up too late and saying in the bathroom far too long. She couldn't get up earlier because she was always up doing her homework until at least midnight as she started it too late because she liked to phone her friends and play on the internet.

Her mum was really angry because she said that Yasmin just wasn't helping herself by getting into a good routine. She was also fed up that Yasmin spent so much time on the computer and they didn't have any time to talk.

In order to make the appropriate changes, Yasmin agreed that she needed to do the following:

- Do her homework at a set time each night eg between 5pm - 7pm.

- Set her alarm for 30 minutes earlier than she was currently doing.
- Agree 'bathroom slots' with her mum and stick to them.
- No more than half hour for internet / phone calls per day in the week (Monday – Thursday).
- Make a 'Talk time' with mum – either during the evening meal / just after this each day.

Joe – aged 15

Joe said that he just didn't want to come to school anymore. He felt thick and stupid because he wasn't getting such good grades as his friends. His mum and dad said that he simply wasn't trying hard enough but Joe said that this wasn't true. He just found it all too much and too hard – particularly English where the teacher just didn't seem to want to give him any help.

On reflection, Joe said that he did waste a lot of time before getting on with his work (phoning friends / watching T.V.) so that when he actually got started on it he hadn't really allowed himself enough time to get the work done properly / to his 'best' standard. He did, however find the English work hard and felt too scared to ask for help in case people called him thick / stupid.

In order to make the appropriate changes, Joe agreed that he needed to do the following:

- Organise his homework time more efficiently and keep to set hours, giving himself a small treat at the end eg watching 'Friends' video at 8.30pm when all the work was completed.
- He needed to concentrate and really listen more in class so as to further help him understand what was being taught.
- Go and see the English teacher privately to say that he was finding the work hard and needed more help.
- Joe also agreed that the Course Tutor could talk to his parents and feedback to them how he really would be trying to work hard and how much he wanted to do well. He would also like to receive more praise from them for his efforts.

Once students have answered this second question in Part 2 of the 1:1 interview, they can then complete the Scaling Activity (Part 3). This activity aims to enable students to measure their own progress and achievements as they can refer back to this towards the end of the 12 week course when completing the Success Check List and Action Plan.

Part 3

The Scaling Activity

Students are required to rate themselves on a scale of 0-10 - 0 would indicate that they feel extremely negative about life in general ñ including school life, 5 would indicate that they feel generally okay but recognise the need to make improvements, 10 would imply that things couldn't be better ie, perfection!)

This rating / scaling system should be explained to students prior to starting the activity. Once a rating has been recorded, students can further reflect upon and identify the following:

- Why I am where I am on the scale?
- Where I would like to be?
- How I can get there ie. What do my own personal targets have to be?

Students will need a photocopy of this Scaling Activity to enable them to refer to the set targets, reinforce goals and what they need to do in order to succeed.

Example

Ellie – aged 15

I am on 3

This is because I feel fat and ugly. I seem to get into trouble for being disruptive and not listening in class. My mum says she's fed up with me being in trouble and looking miserable.

I would like to be on 7 or 8.

I can get there if I try these targets:

- Take more care of my body and do some exercise.
- Eat less fatty junk food.
- Ask my mum to help me with my hair.
- Think before I answer back to the teachers.
- Sit at the front of the class so I won't chat to others and really try hard to do the work.

Resources

The following resources will be needed for the 1:1 interviews:

- A quiet (private) room.
- 1 hour approximately per student.
- Photocopy of the Brief Therapy format (Front covers for the initial 1:1 interview format are provided for both male and female students).
- Photocopy of the Scaling Activity format.

The CAS Course
Initial 1:1 Interview

The CAS Course
Initial 1:1 Interview

Part 1

(a) What is currently going well for you at school? Why?

(b) What is currently not going quite so well for you at school? Why?

(c) What is currently going well at home? Why?

(d) What is currently not going quite so well at home? Why?

(e) What do you think might help you at home/school?

Part 1

(a) The Miracle Question

Imagine that you go to bed tonight and a miracle happens – someone or something waves a magic wand over you and all your problems and difficulties are solved. You wake up to a Perfect Day – at home and at school.

What is different. Have a THINK – how does your day begin and then go on? Talk through what happens on this ideal day/magic day.

(a)What is different to a 'usual" day? Let's think back and list the differences.

The Scaling Activity

Name _____

Year Group _____

The Scale – Highlight where you are now

0 1 2 3 4 5 6 7 8 9 10

Questions to Answer

1) Where am I now?

2) Why?

3) Where would I like to be?

4) How can I get there? What do my targets need to be

Session 1

Completion of self-esteem rating

Session I

- Setting up group rules.
- What is good self-esteem?
- Self-Esteem Assessment.
- Self-Profile and Contract to Change.

Group Session 45 minutes – I hour

At the very start of this session it will be necessary, if not essential, to set 'Group Rules' and focus upon the main objectives of the course. It will be important to create a positive climate and to reassure all students involved that this course will provide them with useful strategies and ideas which will help them to feel better about themselves and to manage themselves more effectively in social contexts.

Course Tutor(s) might highlight the following objectives:
- to provide students with private listening time and space in which to reflect upon their feelings and behaviours
- to help students develop and make use of strategies for building self-esteem, confidence and assertive behaviours
- to encourage students to become more reflective regarding their own situation and to understand that they can effect change
- to encourage students to recognise their right to be who they are and to be accepted by others
- to encourage students to recognise situations, specific events and people who may have a detrimental effect upon their self-esteem and to encourage the development of self-help strategies in order to cope in such situations
- to increase their ability to socialise and co-operate within a group and to support and empathise with others.

Setting the 'Group Rules' will lead on from these objectives. It is very important to allow for students to discuss and agree their own set of rules so as to ensure ownership of them and that everyone adheres to them in each of the following sessions.

These Rules might include:
• we agree to keep our discussions private within the group and not talk about our conversation outside the group *
• we will all try to contribute and think of ideas in every session•
we will not put each other down
• we will try to work together and respect each others point of view
• we will try to be kind to each other and support each other•
no one in the group will be pushed into making a contribution if they don't want to.

It will also be important to be very clear about what it is and is not 'okay' to discuss within this framework. Students should be made aware that if they wish to talk about situations or people who have/ are putting them at risk, then this needs to be done in 1:1 situations with the Course Tutor(s). Also, that the rule of confidentiality will have to be broken should a student disclose any form of abuse as Course Tutor(s) naturally have a legal and moral obligation to try and ensure the safety of students in their care.

The Brainstorming Activity 'What is good self-esteem?' should aid in clarifying a main objective ie. this is what we all need to aspire to. Student's responses might include some of the following:

• liking yourself
• knowing that others like you
• feeling that you can and do achieve
• feeling loved and valued
• being able to co-operate and work with others
• being able to recognise and label good/positive qualities in your-self
• knowing that you can cope and change
• being able to accept positive criticism
• knowing that you are just as good as everyone else
• feeling positive and confident.

Students can work in pairs on this Activity and feedback their responses to each other in the whole group context. Once students have clarified the nature of good self-esteem it will then be possible to complete The Self-Esteem Assessment. It will be necessary to point out the importance of completing the questionnaire as honestly and seriously as possible since this form will clarify exactly where the student feels he / she is now; in terms of confidence, self-esteem and current ability to cope in social / school situations. Students should, on completion of the form, be in a position to highlight 3 areas which they would like to work on and effect change in and to record this information on the Self-Profile Contract to change.

The questionnaire is designed in the style of a Quiz which is common to a wide range of Teenage magazines. It has been adopted from the initial assessment in Jenny Mosely & Eileen Gillibrand's book 'She Who Dares Wins' (Thorsons, 1995).

The questionnaire requires students to rate themselves on the following:

- People liking you / having friends
- Coping with new things and making mistakes
- Trusting and liking others
- Coping with criticism and feeling jealousy
- Feeling misunderstood and excluded
- Putting yourself and others down
- Feeling happy, miserable and or hopeless
- Feeling shy
- Feeling fed up on a daily basis
- Trying to impress and please others
- Feeling that you have missed out and haven't had the same opportunities as others.

Alongside enabling students to highlight areas that they would like to change, this form will also allow tutor(s) to draw up student profiles and to highlight any student who appears to be feeling particularly vulnerable. This could then lead to additional provision (ie. counselling, development of a new approach by teaching and support staff etc) for the individual student. Clearly, any such additional support would need to be discussed privately with the individual student concerned in order to enlist their willingness to co-operate and accept such provision.

Resources

- A quiet room with adequate seating and tables.
- Pens, pencils, rubbers, sharpeners etc.
- 45 minutes – 1 hour to run the session.
- Photocopy of the Group Rules Scroll enlarged to A3 size for Tutor to record student's responses.
- Photocopies of the Brainstorming sheet 'What is good self-esteem?' (enough for 1 between 2)
- Photocopies of the Self-Esteem Assessment – Initial Questionnaire and the Self Profile and Contract to Change for each student (formats have been made available for both male and female students).
- Special folders / files for each student in which they can present all their recorded activities ie Questionnaire, Group Rules, Contract to Change and worksheets and Brainstorming sheets from the following sessions. This record will also help students to evaluate and record their own progress at the end of the course.

Setting Group Rules

Our Rules are:

-
-
-
-
-
-
-
-

Group Rules

- We agree to keep our discussions private within the group and not talk about it outside of the group.

- We will try to think of ideas and make a contribution in every session (if we can).

- We will try not to put people down if they say something.

- We will try to be really kind to each other and support each other.

- No one in the group will be pushed into making a contribution if they don't want to

Brainstorm
What is 'good self esteem'?

Liking yourself

Thinking you are good at things

Work with a partner and try to identify as many definitions as you can. Share your ideas with the group. Do we have similar definitions? Two ideas have been suggested for you.

The CAS Course
Self Esteem Assessment

Initial Questionnaire

Completed by _____ Year Group _____

Self Esteem Assessment
Initial Questionnaire

Please answer the following questions: *Think carefully!*

Tick box A = Never
Tick box B = Sometimes
Tick box C = Often
Tick box D = Always

SECTION 1

	A	B	C	D
Do you think that others like you?	☐	☐	☐	☐
Do you feel that you have "good" friends?	☐	☐	☐	☐
Do you feel that you have good relationships at home	☐	☐	☐	☐
Do you feel nervous when asked to start a new topic in a particular subject?	☐	☐	☐	☐
Can you admit to making mistakes?	☐	☐	☐	☐
Do you think that you are a capable sort of girl? i.e. are you okay at most things?	☐	☐	☐	☐
Are you happy about meeting new people or making new friends?	☐	☐	☐	☐
Do you trust most people?	☐	☐	☐	☐
Can you relax and enjoy yourself?	☐	☐	☐	☐
Do you feel happy in your life?	☐	☐	☐	☐

PART 1 - Now add up your score

A = 1 point
B = 2 points
C = 3 points
D = 4 points   Total = _____

Tick box A = Never
Tick box B = Sometimes
Tick box C = Often
Tick box D = Always

SECTION 2

	A	B	C	D
Do you feel miserable if others criticise you?	☐	☐	☐	☐
Do you feel jealous of other girls and their lives?	☐	☐	☐	☐
Do you worry about what other people think about you?	☐	☐	☐	☐
Do you think that you need to impress others by the way you look?	☐	☐	☐	☐
Do you feel as if others don't understand you?	☐	☐	☐	☐
Do you find yourself in situations where you feel totally excluded from the group?	☐	☐	☐	☐
Do you dislike people (without telling anyone about it)?	☐	☐	☐	☐
Do you tend to keep your problems a secret?	☐	☐	☐	☐
Do you try and please others all the time?	☐	☐	☐	☐
Do you "put yourself down" to others (adults and peers)?	☐	☐	☐	☐
Do you feel depressed about your life situation?	☐	☐	☐	☐
Do you feel that you "miss out" on the chances others get?	☐	☐	☐	☐
Do you make excuses for not doing things that you know you'd really like to do?	☐	☐	☐	☐
Do you feel that your life is hopeless?	☐	☐	☐	☐

PART 2 - Now add up your score   A = 1 point
                                    B = 2 points
                                    C = 3 points
                                    D = 4 points   Total = _____

Section 2 (Continued)

Do you feel that other girls have better relationships than you?

Do you think that you have to try and impress others with the way you act and behave at school?

Do you feel shy or awkward in some situations?

Do you feel 'fed-up' at the end of each day?

PART 2 - Now add up your score   A = 4 point   Total = _____
                                               B = 3 points
                                               C = 2 points
                                               D = 1 point   Overall Total = _____

Results – Score Yourself

Score 28 – 43

You have low self esteem so now you really need to work on it so that you can become a happier and more confident person. START TO THINK POSITIVE: you CAN CHANGE and start to feel good about yourself.

You can begin by making small changes to build a better you and to change not just the way you feel about yourself but how you think others feel about you. Time to go for it girl!

Score 44 – 73

Your self esteem is a bit up and down. You need to start to feel more in control and more confident about your coping strategies. Time to build yourself up and put yourself forward a bit more. Things that may have made you feel a bit fragile before need to be articulated, recognised and swept away. It ís time to clean up and shape up. Go for it!

Score 74 – 102

Your self-esteem is okay but you may still lack confidence in a few key areas. These need to be sorted out so that you can become more confident about who you are and start to really recognise and make the most of all those opportunities. Time to build a bit more! Go for it!

Score 103 – 112

Your self esteem is fine! Top rating! You are generally positive and feel confident about yourself and your life. Set yourself some new goals – make them bigger and better – go for it!

The CAS Course
Self Esteem Assessment

Initial Questionnaire

Completed by _____ Year Group _____

Self Esteem Assessment

Initial Questionnaire

Please answer the following questions: *Think carefully!*

Tick box A = Never
Tick box B = Sometimes
Tick box C = Often
Tick box D = Always

SECTION 1

	A	B	C	D
Do you think that others like you?	☐	☐	☐	☐
Do you feel that you have "good" friends?	☐	☐	☐	☐
Do you feel that you have good relationships at home	☐	☐	☐	☐
Do you feel nervous when asked to start a new topic in a particular subject?	☐	☐	☐	☐
Can you admit to making mistakes?	☐	☐	☐	☐
Do you think that you are a capable sort of boy? i.e. are you okay at most things?	☐	☐	☐	☐
Are you happy about meeting new people or making new friends?	☐	☐	☐	☐
Do you trust most people?	☐	☐	☐	☐
Can you relax and enjoy yourself?	☐	☐	☐	☐
Do you feel happy in your life?	☐	☐	☐	☐

PART 1 - Now add up your score   A = 1 point
B = 2 points
C = 3 points
D = 4 points   Total = _____

Tick box A = Never
Tick box B = Sometimes
Tick box C = Often
Tick box D = Always

SECTION 2

	A	B	C
D			
Do you feel miserable if others criticise you?	☐	☐	☐ ☐
Do you feel jealous of other boys and their lives?	☐	☐	☐ ☐
Do you worry about what other people think about you?	☐	☐	☐ ☐
Do you think that you need to impress others by the way you look?	☐	☐	☐ ☐
Do you feel as if others don't understand you?	☐	☐	☐ ☐
Do you find yourself in situations where you feel totally excluded from the group?	☐	☐	☐ ☐
Do you dislike people (without telling anyone about it)?	☐	☐	☐ ☐
Do you tend to keep your problems a secret?	☐	☐	☐ ☐
Do you try and please others all the time?	☐	☐	☐ ☐
Do you "put yourself down" to others (adults and peers)?	☐	☐	☐ ☐
Do you feel depressed about your life situation?	☐	☐	☐ ☐
Do you feel that you "miss out" on the chances others get?	☐	☐	☐ ☐
Do you make excuses for not doing things that you know you'd really like to do?	☐	☐	☐ ☐
Do you feel that your life is hopeless?	☐	☐	☐ ☐

PART 2 - Now add up your score   A = 4 point
                                            B = 3 points
                                            C = 2 points
                                            D = 1 points   Total = _____

Section 2 (Continued)

	A	B	C	D
Do you feel that other boys have better relationships than you?	☐	☐	☐	☐
Do you think that you have to try and impress others with the way you act and behave at school?	☐	☐	☐	☐
Do you feel shy or awkward in some situations?	☐	☐	☐	☐
Do you feel 'fed-up' at the end of each day?	☐	☐	☐	☐

PART 2 - Now add up your score   A = 4 point   Total = _____
                                     B = 3 points
                                     C = 2 points
                                   D = 1 point   Overall Total = _____

Results – Score Yourself

Score 28 – 43
You have low self esteem so now you really need to work on it so that you can become a happier and more confident person. START TO THINK POSITIVE: you CAN CHANGE and start to feel good about yourself.

You can begin by making small changes to build a better you and to change not just the way you feel about yourself but how you think others feel about you. Time to go for it girl!

Score 44 – 73
Your self esteem is a bit up and down. You need to start to feel more in control and more confident about your coping strategies. Time to build yourself up and put yourself forward a bit more. Things that may have made you feel a bit fragile before need to be articulated, recognised and swept away. It is time to clean up and shape up. Go for it!

Score 74 – 102
Your self-esteem is okay but you may still lack confidence in a few key areas. These need to be sorted out so that you can become more confident about who you are and start to really recognise and make the most of all those opportunities. Time to build a bit more! Go for it!

Score 103 – 112
Your self esteem is fine! Top rating! You are generally positive and feel confident about yourself and your life. Set yourself some new goals – make them bigger and better – go for it!

SELF PROFILE and CONTRACT to Change

Name _Tina_

Year Group _year 11_

3 areas I'd like to change:

- _____

- _____

- _____

CONTRACT to Change

I will try and change by learning and using the new skills introduced in the CAS course.

Signed _____

Date _____

Session 2

Identifying triggers to negative thinking

Session 2

- What is Negative thinking?
- What triggers negative thinking?
- Understanding how Negative feelings affect self-esteem.
- How can we stop negative thinking?

Group Session 45 minutes – 1 hour

This session is divided into 4 main sections as follows:

Defining Negative Thinking

In order to be able to develop coping strategies for any problem it is essential to recognise and understand exactly what that problem is. It may be that many of the students in the group are caught up in negative patterns of thinking and behaviour and that this is a direct result of low self-esteem and confidence.

As with all such 'Brainstorming' activities it is essential that students really do express and articulate their own ideas in their own language. This will ensure that the activity is truly meaningful. Course tutor(s) can record responses onto the Brainstorming sheet provided. These may include the some of the following:

- when you say you can't do something before you've even tried
- when you tell yourself you're stupid, fat and ugly
- when you go somewhere new and you know that people just wont like you
- when you can't believe that someone would do something nice for you and you push them away because you feel so bad.

What triggers Negative thinking?

Students next complete individual worksheets which encourage them to recognise their own 'triggers' to such negative thinking – What makes me think like this?

An example is given on the worksheet which highlights the sequence of event, thought, feeling and resulting behaviour.

Event	Thought	Feeling	Behaviour
My dad left home	It's my fault	Sad	Don't work at school

Clearly, this is not in any sense an easy activity as it highlights very strong emotions and situations which each individual is currently finding very difficult to cope with. It is therefore essential that Course tutor(s) remain sensitive to each individuals needs and ensure that 1:1 time is made available after the session or at an agreed time in the coming week for those students who appear to demand such additional provision.

Understanding how Negative Feelings affect self-esteem

Each student is then provided with a worksheet which focuses upon how what people say about us affects our self-esteem. It may be useful to have some group discussion about this prior to completion of the sheets and to point out the following:

everyone – students and adults alike, can always look back and point out specific events and statements made by significant people in their lives which they have never forgotten and which they know have coloured their view of themselves Eg:

• my dad saying I'm stupid
• my teacher being surprised when I actually passed my exams
• my sister saying I'm ugly
• my aunt telling me to lose weight
• my friend taking my girlfriend away etc.

It is important to recognise how these things particularly 'things that people said' can hurt us and make us feel negative but it is then essential to put these things 'to sleep' and to try and identify ways of coping with them.

This is the focus of the final activity which should hopefully enable students to end on a more positive note!

How can we Stop Negative Thinking?

Again, this Brainstorming Activity requires students to express and articulate their own ideas and strategies in their own language. This activity can be completed in pairs and student's ideas can be fed-back to the whole group in a Plenary session at the end of this lesson. Student's responses / ideas for coping may include some of the following:

Don't blame yourself for things – stop and think if it really is your fault or if there are other contributing factors.

Be honest and say how you feel if and when people upset you. Then it wont build up into a big thing – throw it back at them but admit if you are in the wrong and say sorry.

Turn it into a 'positive' – okay, you feel fat –

well | **Say** | I'm not that enormous
| **Plan** | I'll do some exercise and eat healthier food
| **Do** | Go ahead and do it
| **Tell** | Tell the person who made you feel negative that you've turned it into a positive.

Make a list – write out the negatives and then write out the positives. These negatives might include things that you say to yourself which make you feel down, unhappy or generally bad about yourself or they may be things that others have said about you or to you which have the same end result. Think about what you can say or do in order to cope more positively with such comments and thoughts. Try to change the negatives into positive points for action.

Resources

- A quiet room with adequate seating and tables.
- Pens, pencils, rubbers, sharpeners etc.
- Photocopy of the Brainstorming sheet 'What is Negative Thinking?' enlarged to A3 size for the tutor(s) to record student responses.
- A photocopy of the 'What triggers negative thinking?' worksheet for each student.
- A photocopy of the 'People Said' worksheet for each student
- Copies of the 'How can we stop negative thinking?' brainstorming sheet (enough for 1 between 2).
- 45 minutes – 1 hour to run the session.
- Course tutor(s) may need to have access to a photocopier after or during the session so as to ensure that when students have worked jointly on an activity they then both have a copy of the work completed for their own reference. As usual, all recorded work can be filled in Individual Course folders.
- Student's files for completed work.

Brainstorm
What is Negative Thinking?

What triggers Negative Thinking?

Example:

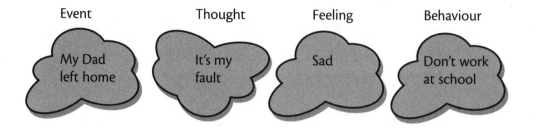

Event — My Dad left home

Thought — It's my fault

Feeling — Sad

Behaviour — Don't work at school

Complete the Clouds! What triggers your negative thinking?

Understanding how Negative Feelings affect self esteem

Me
I said I am

_____
_____
_____
_____
_____
_____
_____
_____
_____

Parents
You are

_____
_____
_____
_____
_____
_____
_____
_____
_____

My
Self
Esteem

Friends/Peers
You are

_____
_____
_____
_____
_____
_____
_____
_____
_____

Teachers
You are

_____
_____
_____
_____
_____
_____
_____
_____
_____

How can we **STOP** Negative Thinking?

DON'T BLAME YOURSELF

BE REASONABLE

BE HONEST AND SAY HOW YOU FEEL

FACE UP TO THE PROBLEM

FIND OUT THE TRUTH

WRITE IT OUT! NEGATIVES AND POSITIVES

Which method do you think would be right for you? Can you suggest any alternative methods? Write them onto the chart.

Go on! Try it out! Be positive!

Session 3

Identifying positive points and practising
Positive Thinking Skills

Session 3

- What are my positive points?
- Moans and Groans: Practising Positive Thinking 1
- Negative Notes and Positive Points Response:
  Practising Positive Thinking 2
- Positive Points Cards

Group Session 45 minutes – 1 hour

This session is divided into 4 main sections as follows:

1. Defining Positive Points

In order to break free of the negative cycle of thinking it is essential for students to begin to identify and articulate the positive qualities that they do have. Initially, this is not an easy activity for someone who is suffering from low self-esteem and it will be essential for Course tutor(s) to remain consistently upbeat and positive about this activity ie constantly reinforce the golden rule: NO NEGATIVES This will essentially be the motto for this session. In order to make this task more achievable students are required to work in pairs. This should allow them to prompt each other and ensure further development of empathy between them.

Positive points might include:

- I can listen well to others
- I am good at doing jobs for my mum
- I have nice eyes
- my hair is shiny
- I am good at telling jokes and making people laugh
- I am a good goal keeper
- I can take good care of things

- my friends say that I am loyal
- I am good at being the referee.

2. Moans and Groans: Practising Positive Thinking 1

This is the first of 2 Positive Thinking strategies which will be introduced to students in this session. This activity requires students to think about and then write out a list of 5 main moans and groans which they know that they continually make or feel. They are then required to turn these moans and groans into positive points. The example given to students is as follows:

e.g. Moans and Groans
- I am in the lowest maths group and I feel thick and people think I am stupid.

Positive Point
- Everyone else is in the same position so we can all help and support each other. Also, the work is the right level for me so I'll learn without feeling frustrated.

The main idea to get across to students is that it is possible to find at least one positive thread in each negative and to draw this out and to create a way forward. This is very much in line with solution focused thinking and an essential skill for students to develop. Students can work on this activity individually and enlist the support of Course tutor(s) as required.

3. Negative Notes and Positive Points Response: Practising Positive Thinking 2

This second positive thinking strategy highlights the fact that we can help each other to overcome and break free of negative thinking. This Activity requires students to work in pairs. Each student records a 'negative note' on one side of their Card and then hands this Card to their partner who is required to complete the 'Positive Points Response' on the reverse of the card.

A Negative note might look like this:

- I am feeling so fed up because in English I am getting such bad grades . My mum says I'm not trying hard but I am. I just don't understand it and I'm sure the teacher thinks I'm thick too.

The Positive Points Response might be as follows:

- You don't need to feel so bad. You need to sort it out. You're not thick. You probably just need some extra help. Why don't you go and ask your teacher about it. Tell him exactly how you feel – I bet he doesn't think you're thick at all and I'm sure he'll try to help you.

Students can then practice 'Acting Out' their Negative Notes and Positive responses by pretending that they are talking to their own reflection in the mirror. (This is preparation for 'Mirror Talk' which is introduced in the next session). Each student states their negative notes to their partner who acts as their reflection and proceeds to respond with the positive points / thoughts, counteracting the negatives. Students then swap over roles and 'act out' the next problem ie. they will both have completed an individual card.

4. Positive Points Cards

Finally, students will be able to make a 'Positive Points Card' for the person with whom they completed Activity no. 3.

Course tutor(s) will have access to an instamatic camera and have 'snapped' the student during the course of this session (preferably smiling!) Each student can then stick their partner's photo onto the Positive Points Card and, referring back to the initial activity (Defining Positive Points) write the positive points into the stars and complete the card. Students can then present these cards to their partners and, hopefully, aid in the process of further building and reinforcing self-esteem and confidence.

It might be a good idea to ask students to 'read out' their partner's cards to the group as a whole as a further reinforcement activity.

Resources

- A quiet room with adequate seating and tables.
- Pens, pencils, rubbers, sharpeners, scissors and Pritt Sticks/glue.
- Photocopies of Brainstorming formats 'Defining Positive Points' for each student (formats are available for both female and male students).
- Photocopies of 'Moans and Groans' worksheet for each student.
- Photocopies on card of Negative Notes/Positive Points Response worksheet for each student. Students can then complete the activity, cutting out the cards and sticking them together back to back.
- Photocopies of the Positive Points Card (on card) for each student.
- An polaroid camera.
- 45 minutes – 1 hour to run the session.
- Student's files for completed work.

Brainstorm

What are positive points? Look and Think

Work with a partner – Can you help each other by pointing out the positives?

Moans and Groans

Practicing Positive Thinking

Think about and write out a list of your moans and groans. Then try to use
POSITIVE THINKING – make a 'positive point' next to each moan and groan.

Moans and Groans

Positive Point

Example:

I'm in the lowest maths group and I feel thick and people think I'm stupid.

Example:
Everyone else is in the same position so we can all help and support each other. Also the work is the right level for me so I'll learn without feeling frustrated.

1)

2)

3)

4)

5)

Negative Notes

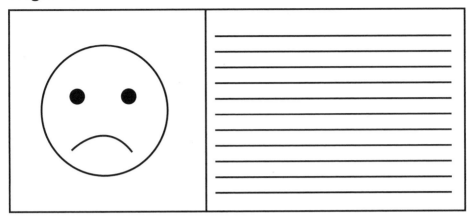

Write your 'negative notes' – Swap your negative notes with someone else in the group: Ask them to complete a 'Positive response' on the reverse of your card

Positive Response

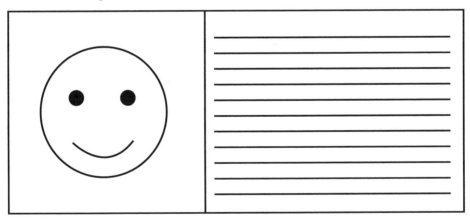

Act it out – Pretend that you are talking to your reflection in the mirror. You state your negative thoughts and the person acting as your reflection counteracts these with positive thoughts and turns your negative notes into positive points. Swap over roles and act it out again.

Positive Points Card

A Photograph of

- -

These are _____'s
Positive Points

Session 4

Using Mirror Talk and Top Talk

Session 4

- What does your 'best' friend do?
- Being your own best friend – Practising Positive 'Top Talk'
- Mirror Talk – Making and Keeping a Positive Pact

Group Session 45 minutes – 1 hour

This session is divided into 3 main sections as follows:

1 What does a 'best' friend do?

For students who exhibit low self-esteem there may be difficulties in formulating and sustaining positive relationships. One key in being able to do this is in recognising the qualities and behaviours of a friend so as to adopt/develop these qualities alongside valuing and perceiving them in those around us. This activity can be completed in the whole group context with Course tutor(s) acting as a scribe and recording student's responses. These might include some of the following definitions as to what a 'best' friend actually does:

- he /she keeps your secrets
- he /she really likes you and is not jealous of you
- he /she doesn't put you down in front of others
- he /she sticks up for you if others pick on you
- he /she helps you with your work
- he /she listens if you have a problem / need to talk and he/ she tries to help you find solutions
- he /she doesn't talk about you behind your back.

This activity will naturally lead on to further discussion around the question: Do friends always do these things and if not, why not?

This is quite a crucial part of the activity as very often students will feel vulnerable in their relationships because they perceived others as 'letting them down'. It is important to focus on the fact that no one is perfect, everyone makes mistakes and it is okay to do so – as long as we recognise the mistake, apologise appropriately and try to make reparation. We need to be able to forgive both ourselves and our friends and to forget our own mistakes and the mistakes of our friends. Also, we do learn from our mistakes so a positive thread can still be pulled out – even from these kinds of relationship problems.

2. Practising Positive 'Top Talk'

Being a good friend to yourself can help ensure the development of a more positive self-image. Students can now be introduced to the concepts of positive top talk and negative 'no' talk and how to move from Negatives to Positives in a structured way, making use of a specific technique.

Students can each complete the worksheet which requires them to identify 4 negative points or negative things that they frequently say to themselves and then formulate a positive Top Talk response in order to counteract and move on from the negatives.

Examples are provided for students so as to ensure understanding and prompt ideas. These include the following:

Negative 'no' Talk
- I am useless at football because I am so slow.

Positive Top Talk
- You can't be good at every sport. Why don't you find yourself another game / activity to have a go at? Try joining a new club and having a go at another sport.

It will be important to emphasise the need to make realistic suggestions which provide for the formulation of achievable goals. Reinforce also the need for students to continually practice this kind of strategy. They might even like to allocate a specific time during each day when they reflect on any negative thoughts and aim to move on from these by practising Positive Top Talk.

3. Mirror Talk – Making and Keeping a Positive Pact

The final activity again reinforces the idea of talking positively or talking 'up' your qualities and abilities. Each student is required to complete the Mirror Talk activity sheet. There are 8 positive statements to complete which are phrased as follows:

- I look good when …
- My goal today is to …
- I can …
- I am good at …
- I feel positive about …
- I feel great when …
- I will …
- I feel happy when …

Students are then encouraged to practice this kind of Top Talk on a daily basis by looking into a mirror and articulating these (or new) positive statements. This is essentially making a 'positive pact' ie. promising to oneself to make use of this strategy on a daily basis – the whole process should only demand 2-3 minutes and it will certainly be time well spent each morning if it ensures a positive start to the day!

Resources

- A quiet room with adequate seating and tables.
- Pens, pencils, rubbers, sharpeners etc.
- Photocopy of the Brainstorming sheet 'What does a best friend do?' enlarged to A3 size for the Course tutor(s) to record student's responses.
- Photocopies of Be Your Own Best Friend worksheet for each student (formats are available for both male and female students).
- Photocopies of Mirror Talk worksheet for each students (formats are available for both male and female students).
- 45 minutes – 1 hour to run the session.
- Student's files for completed work.

Brainstorm
What does a 'best' friend do?

Work as a whole group. Think about the things that good/best friends do e.g. Listen to your problems, keep your secrets, doesn't cuss you or talk about you behind your back etc.

Think! Do friends **always** do these things? If not why not?

Be your Own Best Friend

"Top Talk" – Talking Positive to Yourself

Negative 'no' Talk

Positive Top Talk

Negative 'no' Talk	Positive Top Talk
I'm dead ugly, big and boring	You have lovely brown eyes and very thick silky hair. Why don't you think about using a clear foundation and wearing a new style of clothes. Try taking up a sport to shape up.
I always feel bored and unhappy.	You need to plan a special treat. What would you really like to do/see? Plan it out. Make a list of things that would interest you. Join a club.

Be your Own Best Friend

"Top Talk" – Talking Positive to Yourself

Negative 'no' Talk	Positive Top Talk
I'm useless at football because i'm so slow.	You can't be good at every sport. Why don't you find yourself another game/activity to have a go at? Try joining a new club and having a go at a different sport/game.
I always feel bored and fed up.	Try something new. Give yourself a special treat. Plan out what you can do. Make a list of things that might interest you.

Mirror Talk

Look in the mirror and practice some Positive Top Talk!
Complete the statements in each case.

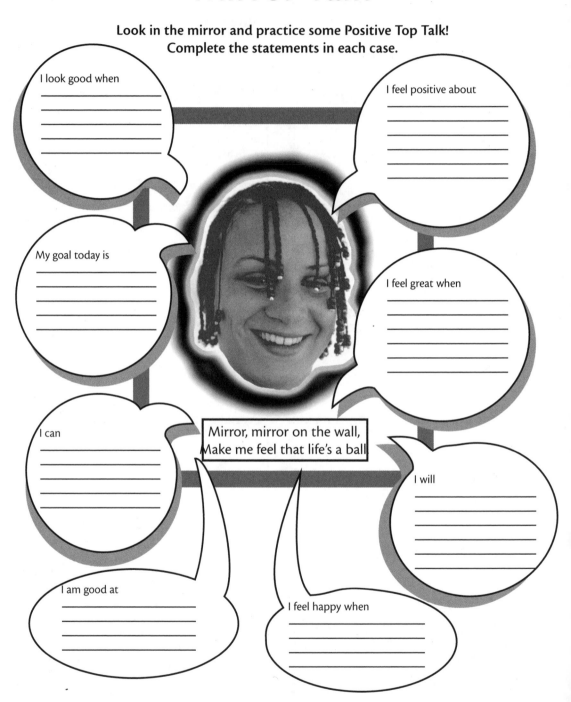

I look good when

I feel positive about

My goal today is

I feel great when

I can

Mirror, mirror on the wall,
Make me feel that life's a ball

I will

I am good at

I feel happy when

Make a POSITIVE PACT with yourself to look in the mirror and say at least eight positive statements to yourself every morning!

Mirror Talk

Look in the mirror and practice some Positive Top Talk!
Complete the statements in each case.

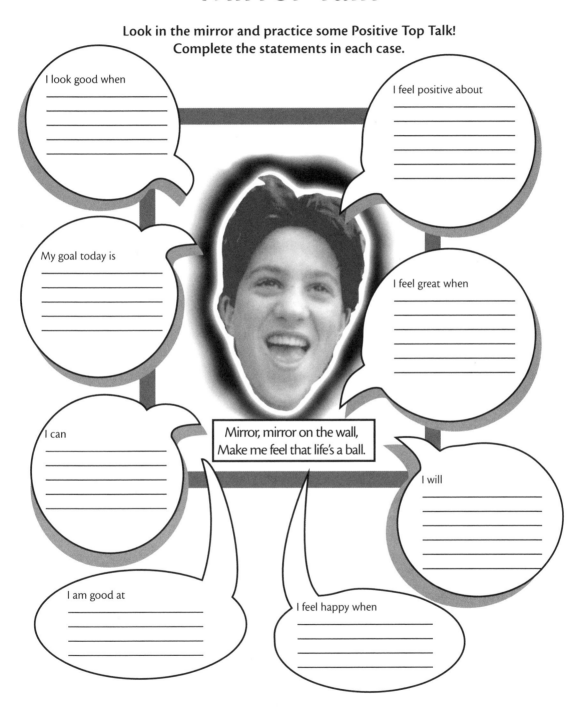

I look good when

I feel positive about

My goal today is

I feel great when

I can

Mirror, mirror on the wall,
Make me feel that life's a ball.

I will

I am good at

I feel happy when

Make a POSITIVE PACT with yourself to look in the mirror and say at least eight positive statements to yourself every morning!

Session 5

Making Action Plans and supporting each other in the process of change

Session 5

- Articulating Positive Changes.
- Super Supporters – how we can help each other to make positive changes.
- Positive Changes – Action Plan.

Group Session 45 minutes – 1 hour

This session is divided into 3 main sections as follows:

Articulating Positive Changes

Students are required to work on an individual basis in this activity and to carefully think about the kinds of changes that they would now like to make in their lives. This will also be an opportunity to reflect on any progress made so far and to reinforce the possibility of making changes for the better.

It will be important that students make realistic and reasonable goals ie. it would not be realistic to say 'I will be a size 10' if you are a size 16 or 'I will be better at English' if you are struggling with basic skills. The goals or changes to be made need to be achievable so as to reinforce and further build up self-esteem and confidence – not to knock back or negate any progress made.

Students can also begin to 'compare notes' on this – it's often reassuring to know that someone is trying to achieve similar goals. Also, this is an opportunity for students to again co-operate with one another and to identify how they can supportive of each other.

Super Supporters – helping each other

Each student can next focus on identifying how they can act as a 'good' or 'best' friend in supporting their peers in making positive changes. They might decide to include some of the strategies taught so far in the CAS Course alongside referring to their partners Brainstorming Sheet and making specific reference to some of the points made.

A student's suggestions for their partner or for their friends in general might include the following:

- I can use positive Top Talk when my friend is being negative.
- I can encourage him / her to use Mirror Talk every day.
- I can make sure we don't eat junk food.
- We can go to the Gym together and support each other in keeping fit.
- I can tell him / her what kinds of clothes suit him / her.
- I can remind him / her to listen to himself / herself when he / she is being negative.
- I can listen or try to feedback positive responses.
- I can praise his / her skills in front of his / her dad.

Positive Changes – Action Plan

Having completed the first 2 activities, students should now be in a position to pick out 5 negatives from the initial Brainstorming sheet which they can now attempt to begin to turn into positives via the formulation of an Action Plan.

This involves the following process:

- listing the 5 negatives which you would like to change to positives
- writing a 'positive point' for each of these negatives
- listing one thing you can 'do' to make the changes
- identifying who can help you and how they can help you
- setting a change date on which to review progress.

One negative might then be presented as follows:

- I'd like to lose weight because I'm fat.
- I'm tall as well so it doesn't look awful and I can play tennis.

- I can eat sensibly and play more tennis.
- My dad and Carl can help me by both playing tennis with me (They like the game too) and my mum can give me a low-fat packed lunch every day.
- I will try and achieve this by 6th November.

Clearly, it will again be essential to emphasise the need to set realistic and achievable targets and to reinforce how positive we must all feel when we are able to identify people who care enough about us to want to help us change.

Resources

- A quiet room with adequate seating and tables.
- Pens, pencils, rubbers, sharpeners, etc.
- Photocopies of the Brainstorming sheet 'What positive changes would I like to make in my life?' for each student.
- Photocopies of the 'Super Supporters' worksheet for each student.
- Photocopies of the Positive Changes – Action Plan sheet for each student.
- 45 minutes – 1 hour to run the session.
- Student's files for completed work.

Brainstorm

What positive changes would I like to make in my life?

Discuss with a partner. Are your lists similar? Can you think of ways that you might support each other to make changes?

Super Supporters

How can we help each other to make positive changes?

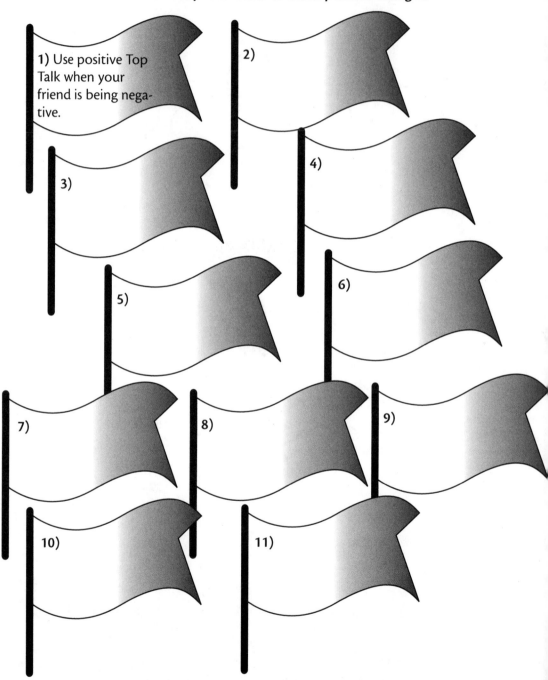

1) Use positive Top Talk when your friend is being negative.

2)

3)

4)

5)

6)

7)

8)

9)

10)

11)

Which one of the strategies do you think will be the best one t use? Why?

Positive Changes
Action Plan

1) List 5 negatives that you'd like to change to positives.

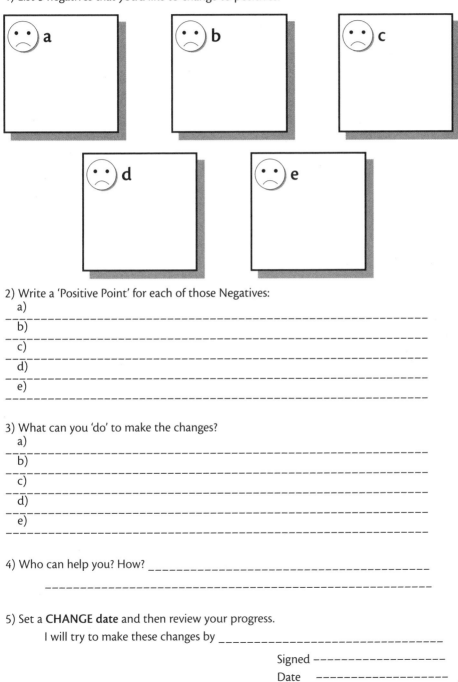

2) Write a 'Positive Point' for each of those Negatives:
   a)
   _____
   b)
   _____
   c)
   _____
   d)
   _____
   e)
   _____

3) What can you 'do' to make the changes?
   a)
   _____
   b)
   _____
   c)
   _____
   d)
   _____
   e)
   _____

4) Who can help you? How? _____
   _____

5) Set a **CHANGE date** and then review your progress.
   I will try to make these changes by _____

                                    Signed _____
                                    Date   _____

Section 6

Understanding the concept of Respect

Session 6

- Defining 'respect' and what we respect about ourselves
- Building on Respect
- This is Me!

Group Session 45 minutes – 1 hour

This session is divided into 3 main sections as follows:

Defining 'Respect'

The use of the word 'respect' is currently very much in vogue and something which the majority of students would regard as one of life's essentials. Some of their views on this topic are summarised as follows:

- you need 'respect' of your peers and family if you are to feel good about yourself
- not to show respect is an insult
- people have to earn respect by behaving in the 'right' way (both students and teachers – but mainly teachers!)
- you need to respect others when they respect you
- to have 'respect' for yourself and your friends is essential, it's like having good self-esteem.

The last contribution probably holds the key to defining what 'respect' has come to mean for adolescents in popular culture. This initial Brainstorming activity aims to engage students in making a variety of definition, alongside subsequently sharing their views within the group as a whole. Students can particularly focus upon the following 2 questions:

• do we share similar definitions of respect?
• do we respect the same things about ourselves?

It might also be interesting to focus on a further question: When should we 'not' show respect? / When do people not deserve to be shown respect?
Student's responses might include:

• when people are racist
• when people try to show you up or make you feel a fool in front of others
• when people steal others things
• when people hurt or abuse other people
• when people lie and get others into trouble for something that they did wrong
• when people grass on you or tell your secrets.

Clearly such a debate touches on major ethical and political issues and should the conversation appear to be particularly useful, it would probably be a good idea to allow some additional time to address these issues. One part of building good self-esteem is in developing the confidence and ability to articulate beliefs and ideas and students should at all times be encouraged to take the opportunity to do this – particularly when in the context of the safe and secure small group.

Building on respect

This activity aims to then support students in building on respect by recognising their own achievements and saying how they feel about them whilst also enlisting the support and views of a friend or partner from within the group in making an additional supporting and affirming comment.
The following is an example of this process:

• a piece of work that you think you did very well – My Novel based on Greek Myths for our Special English Project

- you think – I worked really hard on it and I thought it looked really good because I spent hours on the illustrations
- friend thinks – I loved your chapter headings because each one had a joke in it and I thought that all the stories were very funny-You made what I thought would be boring into something really interesting.

This activity should also reinforce how we can all help and support each other in showing respect and reinforcing each other's self-esteem and confidence.

This is Me!

The final activity in this session aims to reinforce each student's self-esteem and self-respect. Students are required to complete the 'This is Me!' worksheet which encourages and exhorts them to accept and respect themselves. Students are asked to identify 7 reasons why they like themselves and to record them on the sheet. It would also be a nice 'finale' to the activity if students were to read out their responses or swop their sheets with each other and then read each others responses aloud to the group. This will, however, need to be handled with great sensitivity and will be entirely dependant upon how much progress students have made to date. Course tutor(s) will obviously be in a position to assess this. If students feel embar-rassed or are unable to share their responses it might be possible for Course tutor(s) to share some of their comments (not mentioning anyone's name) in a Mini Plenary session at the very end of the lesson.

Resources

- A quiet room with adequate seating and tables.
- Pens, pencils, rubbers, sharpeners etc.
- Photocopies of 'Respect brainstorming sheet' for each student.
- Photocopies of 'Building on Respect' worksheets for each student.
- Photocopies of 'This is Me' worksheet for each student (formats are provided for both male and female students).
- 45 minutes – 1 hour to run the session.
- Student's files for completed work.

Brainstorm

What is 'respect'? What do I respect about myself?

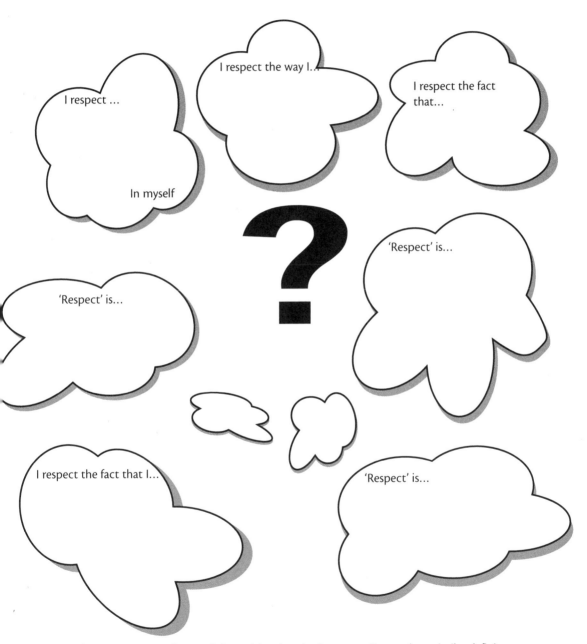

I respect the way I...

I respect ...

I respect the fact that...

In myself

'Respect' is...

'Respect' is...

I respect the fact that I...

'Respect' is...

Work on your own at first, and then with others in the group. Do we share similar definitions of respect? do we respect the same things about ourselves?

Building on Respect

Work with a friend. Say what you think and and ask for their positive point of view

	You Think	Friend Thinks
A Piece of work that you think you did very well.		
Something nice that your teacher said about you recently		
A new change that I've made in myself		
Something kind that I recently did for some-one else		
Something new that I've learnt and gained confidence in		

This is Me!

I like myself because…

I like myself because…

I like myself because…

I like myself because…

I like myself because…

Accept and Respect Yourself

I like myself because…

I like myself because…

I like myself because…

Signed _____

Date _____

Well done! It's good to be you!!

This is Me!

I like myself because…

I like myself because…

I like myself because…

I like myself because…

I like myself because…

Accept and Respect Yourself

I like myself because…

I like myself because…

I like myself because…

Signed _____

Date _____

Well done! It's good to be you!!

Session 7

Coping with stress

Session 7

- Stress check list.
- Making Positive Responses to Stress.
- Coping 'on the spot'.

Group Session 45 minutes – 1 hour

This session is divided into 3 main sections as follows:

Stress Check List

There are times when we all experience some form of stress – either at work, at school or in the home situation and this may exhibit itself in a variety of ways. It is important both to be able to identify triggers to stress and to recognise the kinds of feelings and behaviours that may indicate a rise in our stress levels – then we can start to do something about it.

This initial activity aims to identify if and how students are experiencing feelings of stress. The worksheet details a variety of stress related symptoms and feelings and students are required to tick or cross the statements that they feel apply to them.
These are as follows:

- eating problems
- feeling 'under the weather'
- headaches
- muscle tension
- losing interest in things
- sleep problems
- loss of appetite
- finding it difficult to concentrate

- feeling as though people are getting at you all the time
- feeling irritable
- unable to trust other people
- unable to face the day
- feeling 'over' emotional
- not able to 'switch off' from your thoughts

It will be important to spend some time in discussing positive strategies and ways of dealing with such symptoms prior to going on to the 2nd activity. Also, it is essential that if some students indicate that they are experiencing severe stress levels (ie. they have ticked the majority of the statements) then Course tutor(s) will need to allocate additional 1:1 time at a later stage in order to address these needs. It may also be necessary to refer such students on to outside agencies or in-school counselling services relaying appropriate information to school staff or parents as appropriate.

Making Positive Responses to Stress

The next activity requires students to identify positive responses to stress-related behaviours and thoughts. They are asked to work with a partner in order to formulate these responses. The negative responses are listed as follows:

- deny that you have a problem and it will just disappear
- eat or drink too much in order to feel better
- make excuses for your behaviour or for the way others are acting
- try to change yourself and the way you act in order to fit in with what other people want
- moaning and groaning to everyone about your problems and situation.

Positive responses can be formulated as follows:

- face up to it- say what the problem is and make a list of possible solutions
- don't eat or drink too much – in fact go to the Gym or do extra exercise as this will actually help get rid of some of the tension
- don't make excuses for yourself or anyone else- say it as it is- apologise if necessary and then work out a better way to act

- be yourself – don't try to be what others want you to be or what you think they want you to be- people will like and respect you for who you are if you like and respect yourself and if they don't, just think – I don't need them!
- don't moan and groan – think positive and plan a positive way forward- go and talk about how you feel to a trusted friend or helpful adult-say how you feel and ask for help and advice.

Each pair of students may then like to feedback their ideas to the whole group and it will be interesting to note any similarities and differences in responses and to highlight those that seem to be the most positive and practical.

Coping 'on the spot'

Very often in the school context, students may find themselves in situations of conflict or situations in which their self-esteem is being knocked and they feel unable to cope with the feelings of stress that such situations engender.

This final activity requires them to devise and focus on strategies they can use 'on the spot' or straight away in order to alleviate the problem and reduce the level of stress that they are experiencing. (Students can work in groups of 2-4). Stressful situations can occur very quickly and students may not be in a position to spend time in quietly considering and formulating 'positive' responses. It will consequently be necessary to develop a bank of 'on the spot' coping strategies. For example:

- try to think of something positive or funny
- don't panic-count to 10/20 in your head and take long deep breaths
- don't get into conflict- move away from the situation- get into a quiet place where you can think
- make a mental 'Post it' note- visualise that you are writing the problem onto a post it note and that you have stuck this onto your bedroom wall at home- leave it there and deal with it later.

It will be important for each group of students to share strategies at the end of the session and for Course tutor(s) to prompt all students to make use of these strategies when they next feel that they have or are encountering a stressful situation.

Resources

- A quiet room with adequate seating and tables.
- Pens, pencils, rubbers, sharpeners etc.
- Photocopies of the 'Stress Checklist' for each student.
- Photocopies of 'Making Positive Responses to Stress' worksheet for each student.
- Copies of 'Coping on the spot' worksheet for each group of students to record ideas.
- Access to a photocopier to ensure that each student has a copy of the 'Coping on the spot' worksheet for his/her own file.
- 45 minutes – 1 hour to run the session.
- Student's files for completed work.

Feeling Stressed

Circle ✔ or ✗ for those statements that apply to you.

Making Positive Responses to Stress

See if you can work out the positive responses for these negative thoughts and behaviours. Work with a partner and share your ideas.

Negatives

Positive Responses

Negatives	Positive Responses
Deny that you have a problem and hope it will just disappear.	
Eat/drink too much in order to feel better	
Make excuses for your behaviour or for the way others are acting.	
Try to change yourself and the way you act in order to fit in with what other people want.	
Moaning and groaning to everyone about your situation	

Coping 'on the Spot'

When you know that something or someone is making you feel stressed, but you don't have time to sit down and quietly consider 'positive' responses. What can you do? Work in a group to 'brainstorm' coping strategies. Record your ideas on this sheet – 3 ideas have already been provided.

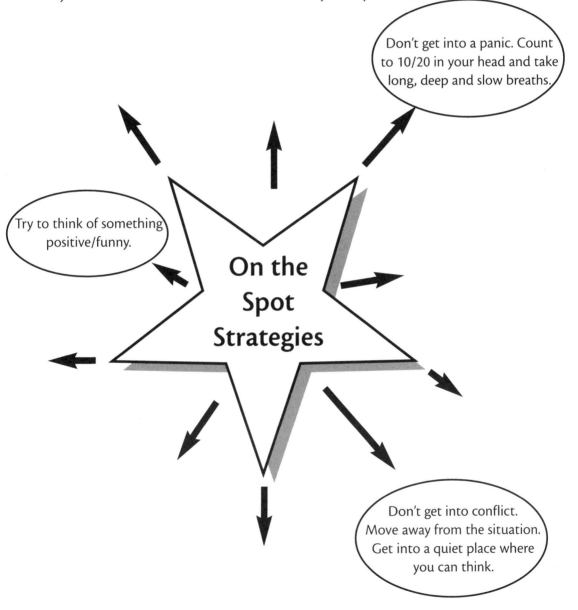

Don't get into a panic. Count to 10/20 in your head and take long, deep and slow breaths.

Try to think of something positive/funny.

On the Spot Strategies

Don't get into conflict. Move away from the situation. Get into a quiet place where you can think.

Test it out!   Practice these skills next time you find yourself feeling stressed out or upset.

Session 8

Understanding the difference between
assertion and aggression.

Session 8

- What is being assertive?
- Being Assertive – Self Check List.
- Practising assertive behaviour – Role Play and use of Situation cards and Assertive Behaviour Skills Top Talk Checklist.

Group Session 45 minutes – 1 hour

This session is divided into 3 main sections as follows:

Brainstorming Session: What is being assertive?

It is not always easy to make the distinction between being assertive and being aggressive. Some students who have low levels of self-esteem may appear to adopt an aggressive stance as a way of dealing with feelings of inadequacy and difficult situations. This is not always intentional. In order to adopt a more positive assertive approach, students need to be very clear about what being assertive actually is – what it means and how it is exhibited in our behaviours. They need to practice these behaviours and transfer them to the real life experiences and emotions that they encounter on a daily basis.

The Brainstorming activity aims to prompt students to formulate definitions of assertive behaviour and consequently to gain a fuller understanding as to what it actually means to be assertive as opposed to aggressive. Students can initially discuss ideas with a partner and make use of a dictionary or appropriate reference materials in order to make a start on this activity.

Definitions might include the following:

- insisting on your rights and knowing your rights
- not being frightened to be honest about what you think and feel

- confidently letting others know your thoughts, feelings and opinions
- being sensitive towards others
- listening to others but making sure that they listen to you as well
- saying what you want
- taking responsibility for your own actions and behaviours and accepting the consequences
- being honest with yourself about what you think and feel
- respecting yourself and respecting others
- don't worry about whether or not people think you are good
- knowing that other people have rights.

Ask students to feedback to the rest of the group once they have completed this task and highlight any similarities and differences in responses.

Being Assertive and Being Aggressive – Self Check List

Students can complete the checklist in which they are required to place a tick next to statements which they know describe them or their behaviour. They can then make some estimation as to how assertive and how aggressive they generally are alongside gaining a further insight and understanding as to the differences between the two behaviours.

The activity sheet asks students to share their responses with another student and to further discuss and articulate the differences between assertion and aggression. They should also ask each other the question: Do you need to be more assertive? And then try to think of ways in which they might achieve such a goal.

Practising Assertive Behaviour

Students will next be required to 'act out' conversations with a partner in which they practice both assertive behaviours and show aggressive behaviours. Situations are detailed on situation cards which students can read through prior to working out the 2 kinds of responses to each situation.

Before formulating these scenes, however, it will be important for Course tutor(s) to provide each pair of students with a copy of the

Assertive Behaviour Skills Top Talk Checklist and to highlight the differences between assertive and aggressive language and responses. The seven examples are given in pairs or opposites.
For example:

- I would like you to stop that …(Assertive)
- If you don't stop doing that I will …(Aggressive)

Students are also required to consider how people actually look when they are feeling or being aggressive or assertive. Do they use a calm voice, a loud voice, folded arms, staring eyes etc. This discussion, alongside reference to the checklist, should enable each pair of students to formulate the 2 scenes making use of appropriate voice, language, body language and content.

Students can then present their scenes to the rest of the group and comment upon the differences between the assertion and aggression scenes. Hopefully, they will also feel confident tackling such an activity at this stage in the course and will also enjoy being stars of the show!

Resources

- A quiet room with adequate seating and tables.
- Pens, pencils, rubbers, sharpeners etc.
- Photocopies of the Brainstorming sheet 'What is being assertive?' (enough for 1 between 2 students).
- Photocopies of the 'Being Assertive Checklist' for each student.
- Photocopies of Assertive Behaviour Skills Top Talk Checklist for each student.
- Photocopies of the Situation Cards (onto card) which should be cut out and laminated prior to the start of the session by Course tutor(s) (Two sets of situation cards are provided so as to allow for specific gender issues to be included. Course tutors can obviously mix and match the cards as appropriate with reference to the make up of the student group).
- Access to a photocopier to ensure that all students have a copy of the completed Brainstorming sheet for their files.
- 45 minutes – 1 hour to run the session.
- Student's files for completed work.

Brainstorm

What is 'being assertive'?

Discuss with a partner. Use a dictionary/reference material to find some definitions.
Share your ideas with the whole group. Do you agree on your definitions?

Being Assertive
Self Check List

Developing Positive Skills – Focus on the differences – be honest.

Being Assertive

- You listen properly to what others are saying.

- You are honest about your thoughts and feelings to others.

- You are honest with yourself about your thoughts and feelings.

- You are sensitive towards other people.

- You ask for what you want

- You take responsibility for your behaviour and the choices you make.

- You don't rely on other people thinking you're 'good'.

- You respect yourself and others.

- You know that you have rights and so do other people.

Being Aggressive

- You are 'loud'.

- You sometimes abuse others verbally/physically.

- You can cause other people to feel upset.

- You need to win even if others get hurt or upset.

- You put others down

- You force others to do things that they don't want to do.

PERSONAL POINT

How assertive are you?
How aggressive are you?
Share your responses with a friend and discuss the differences between the 2 behaviours. Do you need to become more assertive? Start to think of ways in which you can achieve this goal.

Assertive Behaviour Skills

Top Talk Check list

For use in ROLE PLAYS
Use the two lists to help you formulate your responses to situations and distinguish between assertive and aggressive responses. Remember you have to show 2 kinds of responses to each situation.

Assertive Response   Aggressive Responses

Assertive Response	Aggressive Responses
• I would like to stop that…	• If you don't do that I will…
• Can you please listen to me…	• You idiot! Why did you do that?
• What do you think about this?	• You had better change that or else.
• I'm feeling…… about this.	• I can't stand you.
• When can we talk about this?	• What's wrong with you?
• I'd like to do it now…	• Get out of my way.
• I am listening to you so please listen to me.	• You're pathetic/stupid etc.

Think! How do you look when you're feeling/being aggressive/assertive? e.g. Calm voice, loud voice, relaxed, shouting, staring, folded arms.

Situation Cards

Practicing Assertive Behaviour

Work with a partner and 'act out' the conversation indicated in the situation card. Develop 2 scenes:

One in which you act assertively and one in which you respond aggressively.

Three boys in your class keep asking you to go out with them. You don't dislike them but you don't want a 'boyfriend' at the moment.

Your Dad keeps saying that your school work is not good enough and that he thinks you're a bit stupid. He's joking but you feel hurt as you know you are trying as hard as you can.

Situation Cards

Practicing Assertive Behaviour

Work with a partner and 'act out' the conversation indicated in the situation card. Develop 2 scenes:

One in which you act assertively and one in which you respond aggressively.

You are waiting in the lunch queue and 5 boys from Year 9 push in front of you. They smile at you and start to laugh.

Your Maths teacher has given the whole class a detention for talking too much in class. You have to go to the Doctors straight after school so you can't do the detention. Also you feel it was unfair because you weren't talking.

Situation Cards

Practicing Assertive Behaviour

Work with a partner and 'act out' the conversation indicated in the situation card. Develop 2 scenes:

One in which you act assertively and one in which you respond aggressively.

You have been asked to help out at your younger sister ís class party at her Primary School. Your Mum has 'volunteered' you because she knows that you have some time now your exams are over. However, you had arranged to meet your friends in town.

It is Saturday and your Mum has to go to work. You and your brother have been asked to clean the house. When your Mum goes out, your brother says he's just popping out for a quick game of football. He comes back three and a half hours later.

Situation Cards

Practicing Assertive Behaviour

Work with a partner and 'act out' the conversation indicated in the situation card. Develop 2 scenes:

One in which you act assertively and one in which you respond aggressively.

Your friend has said that you've put on lots of weight and that you are looking fat. You feel quite upset about this as she said this in front of a whole group of people in the dining hall.

You are in a toy shop with your younger brother. He accidentally trips over a pile of computer games and knocks them over. The shop assistant seems very annoyed and tells you that you are not responsible enough to look after him.

Situation Cards

Practicing Assertive Behaviour

Work with a partner and 'act out' the conversation indicated in the situation card. Develop 2 scenes:
One in which you act assertively and one in which you respond aggressively.

You had planned to go and see a band with your friends on Saturday night, but your Mum has been let down by her babysitter and consequently wants you to look after your little sister.

You are in a shoe shop looking for some new trainers. One of the assistants tells you off for fiddling with the boxes on the shelf when you hadn't touched them at all.

Situation Cards

Practicing Assertive Behaviour

Work with a partner and 'act out' the conversation indicated in the situation card. Develop 2 scenes:

One in which you act assertively and one in which you respond aggressively.

> **Your friend has just started going out with a girl in Year 8. He spends all his time with her and isn't interested in going out with you. You feel left out and secretly a bit jealous. You also feel embarrassed when he kisses her in public.**

> **When you are walking home from school, four Year 10 boys keep following you and throwing stones at you. You have managed to get away from them so far, but you are beginning to feel stressed by this situation.**

Situation Cards

Practicing Assertive Behaviour

Work with a partner and 'act out' the conversation indicated in the situation card. Develop 2 scenes:

One in which you act assertively and one in which you respond aggressively.

> **Your Mum keeps saying that she can't understand why you're not as clever as your elder brother. She says you're a slow snail – especially at writing. You feel hurt as you know that you always try hard with your work.**

> Other boys in your class keep pushing you from behind when you are lining up to go into lessons and when you go to get your lunch in the dining hall.

Situation Cards

Practicing Assertive Behaviour

Work with a partner and 'act out' the conversation indicated in the situation card. Develop 2 scenes:
One in which you act assertively and one in which you respond aggressively.

Two girls in your form group keep asking you to go out with them. You actually aren't interested in them at all but you haven't been able to get the message across.

You have been given a detention for talking in assembly. However it wasn't you at all – the teacher simply got it wrong. You feel angry and feel like not going to the detention.

Session 9

Responding assertively to Anger

Session 9

- What makes us feel angry?
- Responding assertively to anger – revision of assertive responses identified in Section 8.
- Penny's Problems and Peter's Problems – devising solutions.

Group Session 45 minutes – 1 hour

This session is divided into 3 main sections as follows:

Brainstorming Session: What makes us feel angry?

Coping with feelings of anger in a constructive and positive way is never particularly easy – even if you are a fairly confident person with a good self-concept. In order to be able to respond assertively to people and situations that make them feel angry, students must initially have developed a level of self-knowledge and awareness of what actually triggers their feelings of anger. It is much easier to cope with such difficulties when you have given yourself some emotional priming eg. 'I know that I will feel angry with Mark because he has done nothing but put down Josie since she walked in the room. Consequently I will…' When you know what makes you feel angry and why you feel angry, then you can make use of assertive skills and coping strategies. However, at this stage, the idea is to prompt student's responses to the Brainstorming question.

Students should work individually at first and then share their ideas with the group, identifying any similarities in their responses.

These might include some of the following:

- when people cuss my mum or my family
- when people are racist
- when I can't understand the work
- when people say I'm fat
- if someone puts me down in front of people
- if people shout at me
- when I'm left out and no one wants me in their group
- when people bitch behind my back
- if someone tries to take my friend or my boyfriend away from me
- when my mum won't buy me fashionable clothes
- when my brother calls me 'stupid cow'
- when I forget my homework and the teacher doesn't believe me
- when the teacher won't help me with my work
- when people won't listen to my point of view
- when people let me down and they don't do what they said they would do.

It might also be interesting to ask students to then consider the following question:
Do you think that boys and girls feel angry about the same things? If so, why? If not, why not?

Responding assertively to anger

Ask students to think back to the work completed in the last session and to look quickly at the Assertive Behaviour Skills Checklist and Being Assertive Self Check List.

Many of the situations listed in the Brainstorming session 'What makes us feel angry?' could engender aggressive responses on the part of the students. Ask them to work in small groups and to identify or choose one situation from their Brainstorming List. Then they can attempt to formulate a positive and assertive response to the problem and feed this back to the group as a whole. Such joint problem solving should not only aid in the development of workable strategies but should also further develop a sense of support and empathy between students in the group.

Course tutor(s) could provide an example in order to prompt students in this activity.

For example:

- I get angry when my dad puts me down and says that I'm thick.
- My aggressive response is to shout at him, storm out of the room and cry.
- My positive, assertive response is to ask him not to tease me because it really hurts and it makes me feel unhappy and bad about myself. Maybe he does mean it only as a joke but I can't handle that sort of joke at the moment. I'd really appreciate it if he would stop.

Penny's Problems and Peter's Problems – Devising Solutions

Students can then choose one of Penny's or Peter's problems. These problems have been sent to a problem page ie. Penny and Peter are the Agony Aunt and Uncle who have been asked to find solutions and give appropriate advice. Students are required to formulate their own solutions to these problem page letters, some of which describe feelings of anger, sadness, humiliation or rejection and others which highlight specific teenage problems which require an assertive response. eg. being pressured to have sex when you don't want to.

A Problem Page response sheet is provided so that students can work in pairs in formulating a helpful response to the problem ie, taking on the role of an Agony Aunt. They will need to consider how the student who wrote to Penny or Peter can be assertive and react positively in order to solve his /her problem.

It would finally be a good idea for students to read out the problems and their joint responses to the group as a whole. This will allow for reinforcement of the following:

- the difference between assertiveness and aggression
- the language we use when we are being assertive
- the kind of posture and body language we adopt when acting assertively
- how we can support and encourage each other to develop these skills.

Resources

- A quiet room with adequate seating and tables.
- Pens, pencils, rubbers, sharpeners etc.
- A photocopy of the Brainstorming sheet 'What makes us feel angry?' for each student.
- Student's folders for reference to the last session.
- Photocopies of Penny's Problems and Peter's problems (onto card) Which will have been cut out and laminated by Course tutor(s) prior to the start of the session.
- Photocopies of the Problem Page Response Sheet (1 copy for each pair of students and formats available for both male and female students).
- Access to a photocopier to ensure that all students have a copy of the completed Problem Page Response Sheet for their files.
- 45 minutes – 1 hour to run the session.
- Student's files for completed work.

Brainstorm
What makes us feel ANGRY?

Work individually and then share your ideas with the group.
Do the same/similar things make us feel angry?

Penny's Problems

Dear Penny,

Can you help? I feel so sad. My Mum isn't talking to me because I got such a bad report from school. It's not the way I behave – it's my grades. She says that I'm just not trying hard enough but I really am. She says I'm thick. I feel so angry and sad. Can you help me?

Yours, Trisha.

Dear Penny,

Please help me . My best friend has fallen out with me because I went out with her boyfriend. She won't talk to me now and is starting to get others to gang up on me. I feel really angry. I only went out with him because I felt sorry for him and I don't want to go out with him again. How can I talk to her?

Yours, Alison.

Dear Penny,

I need some help. My friend keeps trying to get me to go out with a boy in Year 9 but I don't want to. He's had lots of girlfriends and thinks he's really something big, but I know that he always tries to force girls into doing stuff they don't want to do. I feel angry and scared. Can you help me please.

Yours, Aisha.

Penny's Problems

Dear Penny,

Please help me . There are 4 girls in my Form group who are really pretty and clever but they are really horrible as well. They keep on saying 'you're fat and ugly' to me and trying to show me up in class if I get the answers wrong. I feel angry and humiliated. What can I do and say?

Yours, Sara.

Dear Penny,

My boyfriend is in Year 11 at my school and I'm in Year 9. He is really nice but he keeps asking me to have sex with him and I just don't feel I want to yet. He says he'll chuck me and find someone else if I don't. What can I do? I feel scared and a bit angry that he is doing this.

Yours, Tammy.

Dear Penny,

My Mum has got a new boyfriend and I thought he was really nice at first but now he is getting on my nerves. He keeps putting me down and everything I do is wrong as far as he is concerned. He says I'm lazy and I don't help out enough at home. He told my Mum I was stupid as well because I only got a level 4 in maths. I'm so fed up with him. I don't know what to do. I don't want to upset my Mum but he is making me feel really angry.

Yours, Karen.

Penny's Problems

Dear Penny,

Please can you help me? I'm so fed up and angry because there are a group of boys at school who keep calling me 'gorilla' and other racist stuff. It's been going on for a whole term and I feel like I'm going to hit them soon – I can't just keep ignoring it. I really hate them. I am black and I'm tall but I'm not going to be ridiculed for either fact. What should I do? I need some advice.

Yours, Cherelle.

Dear Penny,

I went to a party with my best friend last week and she said that she was going to try an Ecstasy tablet. I said I didn't want to and she said I was a whimp. In the end I went home early and left her there. I feel so bad because I know she took one. I don't want to split because I still want to be her friend but I'm scared now. Can you help?

Yours, Melanie.

Dear Penny,

I need some help. My friend keeps trying to get me to go out with a boy in Year 9 but I don't want to. He's had lots of girlfriends and thinks he's really something big, but I know that he always tries to force girls into doing stuff they don't want to do. I feel angry and scared. Can you help me please.

Yours, Aisha.

Peter's Problems

Dear Peter,

I've got a really good friend called Gary who lives around the corner from me. We have been best mates since Primary School and we tend to do everything together. Just recently a new boy has come to our school and he has started calling us gay and telling everyone that we're having sex. What should I do about this?

Yours, Craig.

Dear Peter,

Please help me. My Mum and Dad have recently split up and my Dad has moved to a town which is 350 miles away. Mum says that I can go and stay with him at weekends but my Dad keeps saying he's too busy to have me to stay. I feel like he just doesn't care about me at all now. How can I let him know how I feel?

Yours, Calvin.

Dear Peter,

Can you help? I'm in Year 10 now and I must be the only boy in my form who doesn't wear decent clothes. My Mum just can't afford to buy me new stuff and I feel so embarrassed wearing the unfashionable stuff she gets for me. She doesn't have much money so I can't ask for anything else. The trouble is that people are calling me Tramp Tony. What can I do?

Yours, Tony.

Peter's Problems

Dear Peter,

My girlfriend is really pretty and all the other boys in my class all like her – probably as much as I do. The problem is that I'm starting to feel really jealous and every time another boy goes up to talk to her I feel like thumping him. She's getting fed up with me and says I'm making her feel miserable. I just don't know what to do. I don't want to lose her, but I can't control these feelings. Can you give me some advice?

Yours, Tyrone.

Dear Peter,

Can you help me? I am so fed up and angry because there are a group of girls in Year 9 who keep making racist comments to me. I've told my Form Tutor but that doesn't seem to have stopped it. They keep on and on trying to wind me up. I feel like I'm going to explode and beat them up. What else can I do? Please help.

Yours, Ali.

Dear Peter,

Last week I made a big mistake and told my friend that I'd had sex with my girlfriend. It was a lie, but the other boys were all boasting about how far they'd gone with their girlfriends and I just had to join in and say something, otherwise I would have felt dumb. The problem is he has told everyone in our tutor group and people are calling her really bad names. She is refusing to talk to me and says she'll never trust me again. What can I do? Please help.

Yours, Theo.

Peter's Problems

Dear Peter,

Please can you help? My Mum and Dad are not talking to me at the moment and they have grounded me for 2 weeks because of my behaviour in Maths lessons. They just don't understand that it's not all my fault. The teacher is just so nasty and is always trying to put me down in front of everyone. I feel like it's not fair. Can you help?

Yours, Joe.

Dear Peter,

Please can you help me. My best friend has fallen out with me because I've got a girlfriend. He feels fed up and left out but I can't go out with both of them at the same time as she doesn't like him much. I want to keep on good terms with both of them. How can I do this?

Yours, Carl.

Dear Peter,

I need some help. Two of my friends went with me to a party last week and they were smoking joints in the kitchen. I just don't want to but they said I was soft if I didn't. Anyway, I left the party early and went home. Now they are saying I'm a drip and totally wet. What can I do?

Yours, Ahmed.

Dear

_____

_____

_____

_____

_____

_____

_____

_____

_____

_____

_____

_____

_____

_____

_____

_____

_____

_____

From _____

Problem Page

Dear

_____

_____

_____

_____

_____

_____

_____

_____

_____

_____

_____

_____

_____

_____

_____

From _____

Choose one of 'Peter's Problems and work out with a partner in order to write a helpful response. Think about how the student wrote to Peter can be assertive and react positively in order to solve his problem.

Session 10

Giving and receiving Compliments

Session 10

- How do compliments make us feel?
- Say what you mean – giving compliments to others.
- Personal Compliments Card – giving compliments to yourself.

Group Session 45 minutes – 1 hour

This session is divided into 3 main sections as follows:

Brainstorming Session – How do compliments make us feel?

Generally, those students who do experience low levels of self-esteem may often feel very uneasy and uncomfortable about accepting positive comments or praise from others. They may also thrive on such compliments and demand an inordinate amount of such positive feedback and attention. What is needed is a real balance which enables them to feel able to accept genuine compliments with good grace and to distinguish between praise and flattery.

Students are asked to initially brainstorm this question on an individual basis. Responses might include some of the following:

- happy
- proud
- uncomfortable
- embarrassed
- uneasy
- suspicious
- valued
- frightened that someone might want something
- anxious
- shy – especially if it's from a boy/girl.

It will also be interesting to compare students responses and ask them to explain their reasoning. A key question to focus on is as follows: Are all these feelings positive? If not, why not? Should they be?

Students might like to consider the kind of compliments that make them feel uncomfortable and to identify if there is a need to respond assertively to such attention e.g. sexist 'compliments', compliments which are blatantly untrue, compliments which are intended to gain something etc.

Say what you mean

Students are now asked to formulate their own sets of compliments which they can give to close friends and or family members. A stepped approach is indicated on the Worksheet as follows:

    1 * **Think**   - What do I want to say?
    2 * **Plan**   - This is how and when I will say it
    3 * **Talk**   - Let it out!

This should enable students to quickly formulate honest and genuine emotional responses to friends and family members. The less worrying that is done about the whole process, the easier it will become to overcome any initial embarrassment and actually say what you mean to say!

The compliments are framed for female students to complete as follows:
- You are a good friend because…
- I think your hair is…
- You are special to me because…
- You look…
- You were kind when…
- I love you because…

They are also framed for male students as follows:
- You are a good friend because…
- I think you look good because…
- You mean a lot to me because…
- You look…
- You were thoughtful when…
- I love you because…

Students may wish to give these compliments to the people concerned at a later date.

Personal Compliments Card

This is really another version of Positive Top Talk and is a direct development of the Positive Points Card made use of in Session 3. The only major difference is that at this point in the Course, students are asked to complete their own Compliments Card whereas previously another student had highlighted their personal qualities for them. Hopefully, at this stage, students will have made a certain amount of progress which should enable them to complete this activity. Clearly, however, Course tutor(s) will need to be sensitive to each individual's situation and ensure that additional support and or attention is given as necessary and appropriate.

Each student can complete the card which consists of 10 stars in which they are required to complete the following statement: I am a star because…

Students may wish to respond in a variety of ways and include a wide range of skills and talents that they have developed, alongside personal and social qualities. For example:

- I am a star because I've used Mirror Talk every day this week
- I am a star because I am able to say that I like myself
- I am a star because I know how to be a good friend
- I am a star because I was brave enough to get up and dance at the disco
- I am a star because I stood up to Sasha when she was saying nasty things to me.
- I am a star because I can be assertive
- I am a star because I've stopped feeling so stressed
- I am a star because I'm working harder
- I am a star because I have contributed in a discussion
- I am a star because I've been to badminton 3 times this week.

At this point, it might also be a nice idea for Course tutor(s) to also complete a Personal Compliments Card and share their compliments with the group. It would be interesting to compare student's and tutor's responses – Would they be similar? Are we all working towards similar goals? Do we all need our self-esteem reinforced via positive feedback and compliments?

Perhaps a little 'extra' time might be allotted for such an interesting plenary session.

Resources

- A quiet room with adequate seating and tables.
- Pens, pencils, rubbers, sharpeners etc.
- Photocopies of the Brainstorming sheet 'How do compliments make us feel?' for each student.
- Photocopies of 'Say what you mean' worksheet for each student (formats are available for both male and female students).
- Photocopies (onto card) of the Personal Compliments Card for Students and Tutor(s).
- 45 minutes – 1 hour to run the session.
- Student's files for completed work.

Brainstorm

How do compliments make us feel?

Liking yourself

Thinking you are good at things

Are all these feelings positive? If not, why not? Should they be? Discuss in your group.

Personal Compliments Card

Pay yourself 10 compliments – YOU CAN! Just think, plan and talk!! Write in the stars.

Say What You Mean

Complete the Compliments Speech Bubbles. Imagine that you are saying these things to your friends and members of your family

Don't be shy –
just •think
•Plan &
•talk
1, 2, 3!!

Name...
You are a good friend because...

Name...
I love you because...

Name...
I think your hair is...

Name...
You were kind when...

Name...
You are special to me because...

Name...
You look...

Say What You Mean

Complete the Compliments Speech Bubbles. Imagine that you are saying these things to your friends and members of your family

Don't be shy –
just   •think
         •Plan &
         •talk
1, 2, 3!!

Name...
You are a good friend becaus

Name...
I love you because...

Name...
I think you look good because...

Name...
You were thoughtful when...

Name...
You are special to me because...

Name...
You look...

Session 11

Accepting positive criticism and reinforcement of positive skills

Session 11

- What is Positive Criticism and What is Negative Criticism?
- Dealing with Criticism in a Positive and Assertive way.
- Practice your skills.

Group Session 45 minutes – 1 hour

This session is divided into 3 main sections as follows:

Brainstorming Session – What is Positive Criticism and What is Negative Criticism?

Very often students who exhibit low self-esteem will find it difficult to accept positive criticism let alone distinguish between positive and negative remarks or comments of this kind. All criticism may be seen as 'them getting at me' and usually 'them getting at me again'. However, once self-esteem and confidence levels are raised, it should be possible for students to begin to consider these issues and attempt to clarify for themselves the difference between these 2 kinds of criticism. Also, it will be important to emphasise the meaning of the word 'constructive' and the fact that this implies that whoever is criticising is, in fact, attempting to build you up, to 'construct' a more positive you and not to pull you down.

At this stage, students may wish to opt to work independently on this activity, to work as one of a pair or in a small group. There are no rules on this other than to specify that everyone will be expected to feedback their ideas at the end of the Session. Responses might include:
- negative criticism is given when people really want to pull you down and make you feel bad about yourself
- negative criticism doesn't offer a way forward
- negative criticism makes you feel unhappy and depressed

- positive criticism is given when people want you to succeed by changing the way you do something
- positive criticism gives you a way forward and points you in the right direction
- positive criticism makes you feel a bit uncomfortable at first but that feeling soon goes when you take on board the advice being given to you.

It may be worthwhile providing students with an example of both types of criticism prior to recording ideas on the brainstorming sheet. This will hopefully ensure that all students truly understand the distinction and can begin to distinguish the 2 kinds of criticism for themselves. For example:
- **Negative Criticism** - 'God you're so fat – so much bigger than the   last time I saw you'.
- **Positive Criticism**   - 'You've filled out a bit since the last time I saw you – maybe you should consider joining a Gym. I'll come with you if you like – it could be good fun'.

Dealing with Criticism in a Positive and Assertive Way

This next activity introduces students to a stepped approach to dealing with criticism (positive and negative). The process is as follows:

- Stop and Think – Listen carefully to the criticism
- Wait - Work out exactly what is being said and decide if you think it is true, half true or false
- Go for it – Say how you feel and try to work out a solution. Do what needs doing, then forget about it!

So as to ensure that students really do understand the process, it will probably be necessary for the Course tutor(s) to go through the process, perhaps talking through the examples on the worksheet and reinforcing what the students would need to do at each stage. The example is as follows:
- **Criticism**
  Your mum said that your room is a total mess and that you need to sort it out. She is angry with you.

- **You feel and think**

  Upset and embarrassed. You know that it is half true. Your room looks untidy because you have been revising for exams and there are bits of paper all over the floor. It wouldn't take you too long to tidy it up.

- **You say**

  Okay – I'm sorry, I know it looks bad but it won't take me too long to sort out. I agree that it looks messy but it is not as bad as it seems.

- **You do**

  You tidy it up that evening after school.

Students can then make use of this stepped approach by devising their own 'criticism' ie. a criticism that somebody has made to them, and working through each part of the process, recording their ideas on the worksheet at the same time. These responses and ways of coping can then be shared with the group. It will be interesting to see how many students have or do experience similar kinds of criticism from others.

Practice Your Skills

Finally, there is an opportunity for students to work in pairs and practice this new stepped approach. The worksheet provides 4 examples of 'Criticisms' and asks students to work through this stepped process in order to address each one in turn. During the final plenary session, when students feedback their ideas, it is also essential that Course tutor(s) emphasise the importance of transferring these skills to real life situations.

If we continually practice and make use of this stepped approach to dealing with criticism in a positive and assertive way, the benefits, both socially and emotionally, could be considerable.

Resources

- A quiet room with adequate seating and tables.
- Pens, pencils, rubbers, sharpeners etc.
- Photocopies of the Brainstorming Sheet: 'What is Positive Criticism? What is negative criticism?' for all students (working individually or in small groups).
- Photocopies of the 'Dealing with Criticism in a Positive and Assertive Way' worksheets for each student.
- Photocopies of 'Practice Your Skills' worksheets (1 per pair of students. Formats are available for both male and female students).
- Access to a photocopier to ensure that all students have a copy of the completed 'Practice Your Skills' worksheet for their files.
- 45 minutes – 1 hour to run the session.
- Students files for completed work.

Brainstorm
What is Positive Criticism? What is Negative Criticism?

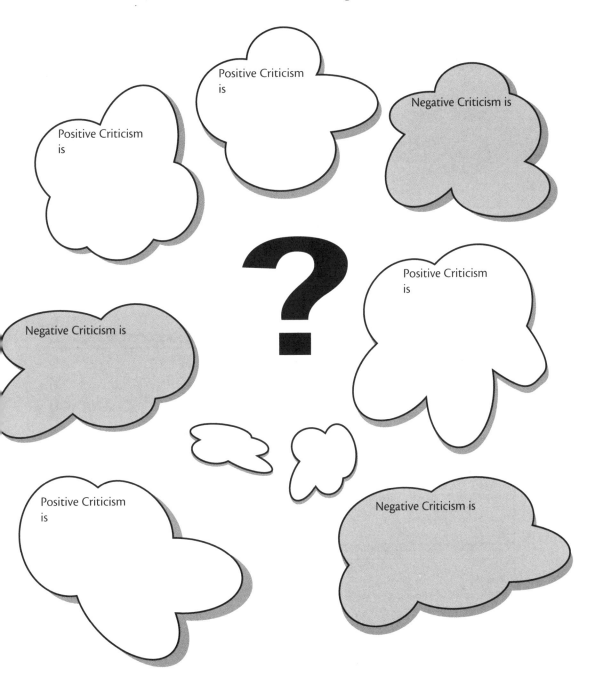

Dealing with Criticism

in a Positive and Assertive Way

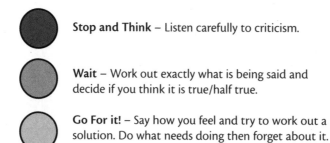

Stop and Think – Listen carefully to criticism.

Wait – Work out exactly what is being said and decide if you think it is true/half true.

Go For it! – Say how you feel and try to work out a solution. Do what needs doing then forget about it.

Example

Criticism
Your Mum said that your room was a total mess and that you need to sort it out. She is angry with you.

You feel and think
Upset and embarrassed. You know that it is half true. Your room looks untidy because you have been revising for exams and there are bits of paper all over the floor. It wouldn't take you too long to tidy it up.

You say
Okay – I'm sorry I know it looks bad but it won't take me too long to sort out. I agree that it looks messy but it's not as bad as it seems.

You do
You tidy it up that evening after school.

Have a go!

Criticism

You feel and think

You say

You do

Have a go! Write in the blank boxes on the sheet. Start with a criticism that has been directed at you and complete the 3 steps. Show how you can deal with the criticism in a positive way.

Practice Your Skills

Work on these 4 examples with a friend. Try to deal with these criticisr
in a positive and assertive way

1. Criticism
Your teacher said that you are not
putting in enough effort with your
English homework. It's poorly presented and you don't bother to check
your spellings.

You feel and think

You say

You do.

2. Criticism
Your friend said that you are always
moaning about being overweight and
it was about time that you stopped
this and actually did something about
it.

You feel and think

You say

You do

3. Criticism
Your brother says that you will never
get a boyfriend because your hair is a
mess and you don't take care of your
appearance.

You feel and think

You say

You do

4. Criticism
The PE teacher said that you could
have made it into the school team if
you bothered to practice more.

You feel and think

You say

You do

Practice Your Skills

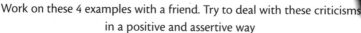

Work on these 4 examples with a friend. Try to deal with these criticisms in a positive and assertive way

1. Criticism

Your teacher said that you are not putting in enough effort with your Geography homework. It's poorly presented and you don't bother to check your spellings.

You feel and think

You say

You do

2. Criticism

Your friend said that you are always moaning about being bored and it was about time that you stopped this and actually did something about it.

You feel and think

You say

You do

3. Criticism

Your brother says that you will never get a girlfriend because your hair is a mess and you don't take care of your appearance.

You feel and think

You say

You do

4. Criticism

The PE teacher said that you could have made it into the school football team if you bothered to practice more.

You feel and think

You say

You do

Session 12

Course Review and Evaluation
Looking to the Future

Session 12

- What have we learnt from the CAS Course?
- CAS Course Success Checklist.
- CAS Course Action Plan.
- Certificates of Completion.

Group Session 45 minutes – 1 hour

This session is divided into 3 main sections as follows:

Brainstorming Session – What have we learnt from the CAS Course?

This last session of the course should, hopefully, allow for a real celebration of achievement. It will naturally be important to ensure that every student is able to honestly articulate some progress and improvement in coping strategies. This is also an opportunity to ensure that everyone is absolutely clear as to what has actually been covered and how to make use of all the skills and strategies learnt.

Initially, students can work with a partner on this activity prior to feeding back their ideas to the rest of the group. Alongside having learnt to make use of the techniques taught, it is also hoped that student's responses will also include personal views and feelings i.e. I have learnt to like myself, I have learnt that people like me!

Responses relating to concepts covered in the Course may include the following:

- positive thinking skills
- recognition of negative responses from others and within oneself
- turning moans and groans into positive points
- recognition of one's own positive points
- understanding what makes a good friend

- understanding that everyone is allowed to make mistakes
- knowing that everyone has 'rights'
- able to help others cope better with negative feelings
- using Mirror Talk and Top Talk
- recognising things that need to be changed in oneself
- accepting and respecting oneself
- showing respect for others
- using strategies to cope with stress
- being assertive in a positive way
- able to give and accept compliments
- responding assertively to anger or situations that make you feel angry
- saying what you mean
- recognising the difference between positive and negative criticism
- coping assertively with positive criticism.

Students should, after having completed this activity, be in a good position to then individually complete the CAS Course Success Checklist.

CAS Course Success Check List

Students are asked to assess their skills by placing a tick in the appropriate box next to each statement. Statement are all phrased positively i.e. I can think positively, I can recognise my positive points etc and students are asked to tick one of three boxes: always, sometimes or never.

Once the form is completed, it provides an opportunity for both the students and the Course tutor(s) to really evaluate progress alongside highlighting key areas for future work. The latter will form the basis for completion of the Action Plan.

It should, of course, also be possible to determine which students require further additional support now that the weekly group sessions have come to an end. It is probable that the majority of students would benefit from regular Mentoring sessions (as discussed in the introduction to the course) for at least a half- term or term. There may also be some students who require additional specialist provision and this needs to be brought to the attention of Parents or Carers in consultation with the students concerned. (This should not come as a 'shock' to Parents or Carers if regular liaison structures are in place).

CAS Course Action Plan

Students complete the Action Plan, highlighting 4 areas that they still need to work on and formulating 4 specific targets. Clearly these need to be disseminated to all involved Staff and Parents or Carers and can, if appropriate, be incorporated into the students I.E.P. (Individual Education Plan) or IBP (Individual Behaviour Plan)

Certificates of Completion

All students will receive a Certificate of Completion. It would also be a nice idea to celebrate with some music, food and drink i.e., Why not have a small party and end the whole Course on a really celebratory note!

Resources

- A quiet room with adequate seating and tables.
- Pens, pencils, rubbers, sharpeners etc.
- Photocopies of the Brainstorming sheet 'What have we learnt from the CAS Course?' (1 between each pair of students).
- Photocopies of the CAS Course Success Check List for each student.
- Photocopies of the CAS Course Action Plan for each student.
- Photocopies (onto card) of the Certificate of Completion for each student. These should have been filled in and laminated prior to the start of the session (formats are available for both male and female students).
- Access to a photocopier to ensure that students have a copy of the completed Brainstorming Sheet for their files.

Brainstorm
What have we learnt from the CAS Course?

Work with a partner. Try to identify the strategies and skills that we have covered in the sessions. Share your ideas with the group.

Self Esteem Assessment
Check List

Please assess your skills by placing a tick in the appropriate box next to each statement.   Think carefully!

Statement	Always	Sometimes	Never
I can think positively.	☐	☐	☐
I can recognise what makes me feel negative.	☐	☐	☐
I can turn moans and groans into 'Positive points'.	☐	☐	☐
I can recognise my positive points.	☐	☐	☐
I can help others cope better with negative thinking.	☐	☐	☐
I can recognise when someone is being a good friend.	☐	☐	☐
I can use 'Mirror Talk' to make myself feel good.	☐	☐	☐
I can use 'Top Talk' to turn negatives into positives.	☐	☐	☐
I can recognise things I need to change about myself.	☐	☐	☐
I can respect and accept myself.	☐	☐	☐
I can show respect for others.	☐	☐	☐
I can use strategies to cope with stress.	☐	☐	☐
I can be assertive in a positive way.	☐	☐	☐

CAS Course Success Check List Continued...

Statement	Always	Sometimes	Never
I can respond assertively to anger.	☐	☐	☐
I can accept compliments.	☐	☐	☐
I can give compliments to others	☐	☐	☐
I can say what I really mean.	☐	☐	☐
I can recognise the difference between positive and negative criticism.	☐	☐	☐
Total Ticks	☐	☐	☐

Look carefully! what have you learnt? What do you still need to work on? Think and plan. Complete your Personal Action Plan.

CAS Course Action Plan

Be Positive

Look back at the success list and identify 4 areas that you still need to work on.

Look to the Future

I still need to work on.

I will...

I will...

I will...

I will...

I will ask...

To help me achieve these targets.

Signed

Date

Review Date

Certificate of Completion

You have successfully completed the
CAS Course

Well Done

You are a Star!

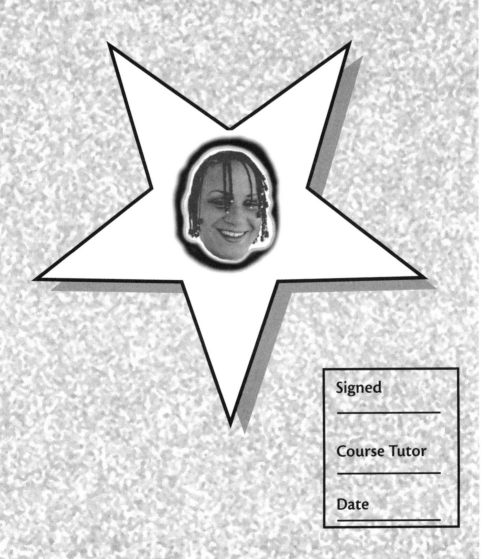

Signed
_____

Course Tutor
_____

Date
_____

Certificate of Completion

You have successfully completed the
CAS Course

Well Done

You are a Star!

Signed
_____

Course Tutor
_____

Date
_____

Follow on work and mentoring form

Follow on Work

In the introduction to this course it was clearly stated that students who have been involved in the CAS Course group would continue to need some form of support after the course had finished. For some students it may be necessary to involve an outside agency in order to build on and further develop the work which has been initiated through these sessions. Such students will need to be identified via the usual school systems for working with students identified as having special educational needs.

However for all students involved in the course it is essential that a follow up meeting is organised in order to reflect on and evaluate progress and to identify any continuing needs. It is crucial that once students have been supported in this way that institutions continue to provide opportunities to ensure that students' needs continue to be met. As stated in the introduction this will call for a whole school approach to developing a listening time policy. Students readily respond to a miracle question but what we as educators should of course realise is that there are no miracle cures and affecting student behaviour is a long term commitment. Schools need to see that this kind of programme is merely a start in the development of a positive approach to ensuring the inclusion of students with emotional and behavioural difficulties and low self-esteem. Staff need to accept and allow for the fact that students will respond differently to this kind of intervention and that some may require an opportunity to reinforce and revisit the learnt skills if or when things go wrong for them. To ignore such students would be counterproductive. Any successes need to be built on and be celebrated. Even when things go wrong it will always be possible to re-establish and maintain the positive, solution focused approach.

In the follow up meetings students can review action plans and again make use of the scaling activity. New targets can be set and incorporated into IEPs. This meeting can also provide an opportunity to share and celebrate successes and confirm positive relationships.

The Mentoring Scheme

At the start of this course it was suggested that schools may wish to implement a mentoring scheme to run alongside the CAS Course. Such a system would allow for students to work consistently with a significant adult in the school context with whom they could build a trusting and positive relationship. This would also allow for the regular setting of appropriate, achievable targets and for the student to become more reflective and develop a greater range of strategies. So if things go wrong it should always be possible to re-establish and maintain the positive, solution focused approach.

A suggested format for recording a weekly mentoring session is included. This form initially asks the student to make use of the scaling activity as detailed in the student interview/introduction session. Students awarding themselves 0 would imply that they feel extremely negative about the week, 5 would imply that they felt OK but recognised the need to make further improvement and 10 would imply that the student had experienced a perfect week!

Secondly, the student should reflect back on the previous week identifying both positives and negatives. This further develops the solution focused approach in that the student is asked not only to identify any problems and how they dealt with them but also to suggest what they could have done differently i.e. what would be a more positive response next time.

The third section on the monitoring form requires both the student and the mentor to agree whether or not targets have been achieved and to record the type of support currently on offer to the student e.g. time out facility, use of homework club, alternative counselling provision etc.

The fourth section requires the student and mentor to agree and record targets for the coming week and to identify the date and time of the next meeting. Students need to specify the rating that they would then like to achieve during the coming week. Naturally, every aspect of this process is crucial but perhaps the most vital part of the whole process is for mentors to provide positive feedback and recognise the student's progress in the weekly feedback call to parents/carers. Such a system would and should clearly reinforce how all involved adults are supporting the student in a positive way and working in partnership in the best interests of the student. This could also provide an opportunity for staff and parents/carers to ensure a consistent approach and programme for the student which significantly links the two of the most important aspects of the student's life at school and home.

Mentoring Scheme Weekly Record form

Name   D.O.B.

Tutor Group   date of meeting

Pupil Weekly Rating   /10

Pupil's Views
How has this week been (good things and bad things)
Did you have any difficulties? How were they dealt with? Could you have done anything differently?

Reviewing targets – Pupil and Mentor comments

Have targets been achieved? What support has been offered?

Targets for the coming week. Pupil and Mentor to agree.

-
-
-
-

Next meeting   date   time

Next week I would like to achieve a score of   /10

Weekly feedback call to Parents/Carers

Date / Time of next call